T0110526

Cambridge Elements ☰

Elements in Histories of Emotions and the Senses
edited by
Rob Boddice
Tampere University
Piroska Nagy
Université du Québec à Montréal (UQAM)
Mark Smith
University of South Carolina

SENSORIUM

Contextualizing the Senses and Cognition in History and Across Cultures

David Howes
Concordia University and McGill University

CAMBRIDGE
UNIVERSITY PRESS

Shaftesbury Road, Cambridge CB2 8EA, United Kingdom

One Liberty Plaza, 20th Floor, New York, NY 10006, USA

477 Williamstown Road, Port Melbourne, VIC 3207, Australia

314–321, 3rd Floor, Plot 3, Splendor Forum, Jasola District Centre,
New Delhi – 110025, India

103 Penang Road, #05-06/07, Visioncrest Commercial, Singapore 238467

Cambridge University Press is part of Cambridge University Press & Assessment,
a department of the University of Cambridge.

We share the University's mission to contribute to society through the pursuit of
education, learning and research at the highest international levels of excellence.

www.cambridge.org
Information on this title: www.cambridge.org/9781009517225

DOI: 10.1017/9781009329668

First published 2024

A catalogue record for this publication is available from the British Library.

ISBN 978-1-009-51722-5 Hardback
ISBN 978-1-009-32968-2 Paperback
ISSN 2632-1068 (online)
ISSN 2632-105X (print)

Sensorium

Contextualizing the Senses and Cognition in History and Across Cultures

Elements in Histories of Emotions and the Senses

DOI: 10.1017/9781009329668
First published online: April 2024

David Howes
Concordia University and McGill University

Author for correspondence: David Howes, david.howes@concordia.ca

Abstract: Do the senses have a history? How many might there be? Are the senses so many independent channels, or do they interact with and modulate each other? If so, how might we cultivate the capacity to see feelingly or hear colours? What makes smell 'the affective sense'? These are among the questions to be addressed in this Element. It pries the senses and perception loose from the psychology laboratory to focus on how they have been constructed and lived differently in different historical periods and across cultures. Many of its findings are surprising because they run counter to our common-sense assumptions about the sensorium. They make uncommon sense. Plus the reader will meet some fascinating historical characters like the prolific 17th century natural philosopher Margaret Cavendish (also author of the play *The Convent of Pleasure*) and the late 19th century artist James McNeill Whistler, who infused his paintings with music.

This Element also has a video abstract: www.cambridge.org/David

Keywords: sensory history, sensory anthropology, psychology of perception, cognitive psychology, multisensory aesthetics

ISBNs: 9781009517225 (HB), 9781009329682 (PB), 9781009329668 (OC)
ISSNs: 2632-1068 (online), 2632-105X (print)

Contents

Prologue: Sensory Openings

How many senses are there, really? Is it the eyes that see, or the mind? Do the senses have a history? What makes smell 'the affective sense' par excellence? Are the senses so many independent channels, or do they interact and modulate each other? And, if so, how might we cultivate the capacity to smell colours or see feelingly?

These are among the questions to be addressed in this Element. It pries the senses and perception loose from the psychology laboratory (where their study has come to be confined in modernity) to focus on how they have been constructed and lived differently in different historical periods and across cultures. Many of its findings are surprising because they run counter to our common-sense assumptions about the sensorium. They make uncommon sense.

Part I is called 'Explorations'. Section 1 looks into the issue of the enumeration of the senses, or how the sensorium gets divided up. As we shall see, in many traditions there is a link between the anatomy of the senses and the structure of the cosmos – sensory anatomy and sensory cosmology are one. From this holistic perspective, it emerges that the senses are mediators, or dynamic mediums, rather than passive receptors localized in the body. Other shifts follow, such as from physiology to practice or 'technique'. Section 2 delves into the techniques of hearing, Section 3 explores diverse ways of smelling, and Section 4 enucleates - that is, draws out the gist of - the interrelationship between seeing and feeling.

Part II is called '*Études Sensorielles*'. It offers a pair of case studies in the history of the senses. Section 5 has the scientific revolution of the seventeenth century as its backdrop, when the senses were instrumentalized and harnessed to reveal nature's secrets. The focus in this section is on the natural philosophy and the vast literary output (including poems and plays and the first ever science fiction novel) of Margaret Lucas Cavendish (1623–73), Duchess of Newcastle. The section will show how her sensuous epistemology and vital materialist ontology countered the mechanical materialism of her male peers, who arrogated doing science to their sex alone. Cavendish was sharply critical of gender segregation in science and society alike. Her insistence on emancipation in place of domination warrants serious consideration from the sensory and social studies perspective advocated in this Element.

Section 6 has the artistic ferment of the late nineteenth century as its backdrop. The section offers a sensory biography of the works and life of the expatriate American painter James McNeill Whistler (1834–1903). It will show that the key to his genius lay in the way he crossed geographical, cultural and sensory borders in his artistic practice. The Element concludes with a plea for 'leading with the senses' (in place of cognition or representation) in the study of mind, society and cosmos, the better to sense – and make sense of – whatever may emerge.

Part I Explorations

1 Making Senses: On How the Sensorium Gets Divided

> Sight, hearing, smell, taste and touch: that the senses should be enumerated in this way is not self-evident. The number and order of the senses are fixed by custom and tradition, not by nature. The regular order being subject to occasional change proves its arbitrariness.
>
> —Louise Vinge

How many senses do we actually possess? I am often asked this question when I give a talk. In *De Anima* (*On the Soul*), the philosopher Aristotle (n.d.) famously proclaimed the senses to be five in number. But even those who have never read Aristotle know about the five-sense model. Perhaps they were exposed to one of the many children's books on 'the five senses'. Most of these books are picture books;[1] some are multimodal (e.g., they have fluffy, smooth or other textured patches that you can feel). Some have amusing titles, like *You Can't Taste a Pickle With Your Ear!* (Ziefert 2014). They are all meant to be educational, and so, for those raised in this tradition, the notion of there being five senses comes to seem like common sense.

The more scientifically informed members of an audience will, however, observe that there are more than five senses, that Aristotle left out proprioception (the awareness of one's own body in space) and kinaesthesia (muscle sense), for example. These senses were not definitively identified until the nineteenth century. As Zeynep Çelik notes:

> Kinaesthesia, the sense of bodily movement, had been studied before the nineteenth century under a variety of other names, including 'inner sense' and 'organic' or 'visceral' sensibility – all referring to those unclassifiable sensations that could not be traced accurately to one of the five known sense organs, but seemed to originate from the undifferentiated mass of the viscera. It was not until the early nineteenth century, however, that 'muscle sense' was officially declared a 'sixth sense' in its own right. (Çelik 2006: 159)

---

[1] By way of example, consider *Super Senses* (1996), a SNAPSHOT™ Book: 'Young readers choose a tab, pick a page, and discover what's behind the symbols.' The five tabs each feature a picture of a different sense organ. Open the tab for the ear and there are pictures of a duck (with the words 'quack quack'), a clock ('tick tock'), a fire engine ('oooo oooo'), an old-fashioned rotary dial telephone ('ring ring') and so on. The display for touch is not so soundful: it features pictures of sticky honey (dripping from a spoon), soft feathers, hard pebbles, a spiky cactus and an ice popsicle.

Sensory scientists will object that the list does not stop at six, that thanks to advances in neurobiology we now know that there are at least ten senses, but more likely twenty-one, and radical estimates put the number as high as thirty-three (Durie 2005). These enumerations are arrived at when all of the 'intero ceptive' senses (keyed to discriminable receptors) and 'exteroceptive' senses (more fragmented than is commonly thought) are counted together (see Howes 2022a: 82–3; DeSalle 2018).

Moving beyond Western traditions, how many senses have other cultures counted? This is a fascinating topic with surprising variations. Before broadening our scope, however, let us undertake an 'archaeological' excursion into the history of ideas about the senses in the West.

Archaeology of the Sensorium

Starting with Aristotle, we find that the senses were not simply anatomical, they were cosmological. According to the Aristotelian worldview, the universe was composed of four elements: Earth, Air, Fire and Water. Each element was distinguished by a different combination of qualities: the wet, dry, hot and cold. Thus, Earth was classified as cold and dry, Water as cold and wet, Fire as hot and dry, and Air as hot and wet.

The senses were further understood to be distinguishable by reference to the four elements. According to Aristotle, Water was the element of sight (because the eye contains water); Air was the element of hearing; Fire, the element of smell; and Earth, the element both of touch and of taste, due to the latter being classified as 'a mode of touch' (Connor 2015: 241). This cosmic understanding contrasts with the modern understanding of the senses as localized in their corresponding bodily organ (eye, ear, nose, etc.).

Each sense was supposed to have its 'proper sensible', such as colour in the case of sight, sound in the case of hearing and odour in the case of smell. The provincialism of this categorization posed certain difficulties, though. For example, what of those objects that are perceived by more than one sense, such as figure or number, which are discernible by sight and by touch? (Aristotle called these qualities the 'common sensibles'.) What of complex sensations, such as the experience of eating an apple, which is both red and sweet? Furthermore, given that a sense cannot perceive itself, how is it that we perceive *that* we see and hear?

In answering these questions, Aristotle reasoned that there must be a further sense, a shared sense, responsible for distinguishing, coordinating and unifying the five senses and their deliverances. This power he called 'the common sense' (*koinē aisthēsis*, or *sensus communis* in Latin translation). This sense sounds suspiciously like a sixth sense. Was Aristotle contradicting himself? No, for as Daniel Heller-Roazen explains in *The Inner Touch: Archaeology of a Sensation*:

> Strictly speaking, the common sense [on account of its commonality and irreducibility] is ... not a sixth sense, ... it is nothing other than the sense of the difference and unity of the five senses, as a whole: the perception of the simultaneous conjunction and disjunction of sensations in the common sensible, the complex sensation, and finally, the self-reflexive perception [or sense of oneself sensing]. (Heller-Roazen 2007: 35)

In the third century, the theologian Origen introduced the idea of 'spiritual senses' corresponding to the physical ones. 'According to Origen these senses enabled one to perceive transcendental phenomena, such as the "sweetness" of the word of God' (Classen [1993a] 2023: 3) or having a 'vision' (Gavrilyuk and Coakley 2011; Canévet et al. 1993). The doctrine of the spiritual senses was complemented by the elaboration of a model of the 'inner senses', which included memory, imagination, cogitation and the common sense of Aristotle. It bears underlining that all of these powers were conceptualized as sensory faculties, not cognitive capacities.[2] They were continuous with the world rather than independent of it, much less opposed to it, as in the way imagination, in particular, is understood today (Kearney 1988).

Moving into the modern age, the eighteenth century was a particularly fertile period for the identification of novel sensory faculties. This period is commonly referred to as the Enlightenment (*siècle des lumières* in French), the Age of Reason or (somewhat surprisingly in view of the close association between luminescence or lucidity and rationality) the Age of Sensibility. The last term, 'sensibility', has a subjective, emotional and somewhat murky tinge that conflicts with the ostensible objectivity and universality of reason. It has more to do with feeling than with thinking. However, Enlightenment thinkers, especially those of the Scottish Enlightenment (Hutcheson, Hume, Smith, Sir William Hamilton), thought a lot about feeling and, in particular, social feelings. They coined a number of senses that were classified as 'inward' but also eminently social. For example, the political philosopher James Moore observes that Frances Hutcheson, in *An Inquiry into the Original of Our Ideas of Beauty and Virtue* (1725), posited a sixth, moral sense which, Hutcheson claimed,

> brings to mind an idea of virtue whenever one perceives a character or an action prompted by benevolence, kind affection or public spirit. He considered the moral sense analogous to the sense of beauty, a seventh sense,

---

[2] This is because memory, imagination and so on belonged to the sensitive soul in humans, as distinct from the rational soul (our cognition) and the nutritive soul, responsible for the vitality of humans (and animals and plants).

which brings before the mind an idea of beauty when it perceives uniformity in variety in compositions, landscapes, works of art and the order of the world. . . . In another work, . . . [Hutcheson] added an eighth sense, a public sense or a determination to be pleased with the happiness of others and uneasy at their misery. (James Moore, personal communication)[3]

The list continues with such other senses as the sense of honour (a ninth sense) and common sense (the way we moderns understand this notion, not Aristotle),[4] which makes ten. It will be observed that all of these senses (without organs) were basically social constructions.

During the nineteenth century, numerous interoceptive senses came to be identified, such as proprioception and kinaesthesia, as discussed earlier. The *milieu intérieur* expanded exponentially, thanks to advances in physiology (Paterson 2021). The sensorium also underwent a second spiritual revolution (redoubling Origen's intervention). The Spiritualists (Madame Blavatsky, Charles Webster Leadbeater) posited various occult powers, such as telepathy and communicating with the souls of the departed. Diverse learned societies were formed to investigate these powers, notably the British Society for Psychical Research (founded in 1882). They sought to 'scientize' the occult powers of the Spiritualists, and reclassified these powers as 'psychic' (Thurschwell 2001).

The drive to scientize or 'psychologize' the Spiritualist sensorium culminated in the invention of the notion of 'extrasensory perception', or ESP, as proposed by the Duke University psychologist J. B. Rhine (1934). The field of 'parapsychology' was thus born. The science of statistics was pressed into service and numerous ingenious experiments, such as Zener cards,[5] were developed to sift psychic fact from fiction, or chicanery. A new, more psychological-sounding language was invented to describe these proclivities: premonitions were reclassified as 'precognition', clairvoyance as 'remote-viewing' and levitation as 'psychokinesis'.

Thus, the notion of 'the five senses' has by no means been the only way of dividing up the sensorium in Western history (*pace* Aristotle). In addition to the canonical five senses, there are the inner, the spiritual, the inward or social, the

---

[3] James Moore is a political philosopher at Concordia University (now retired). I am indebted to him for having enlightened me regarding the social senses of the Scottish Enlightenment over the course of numerous memorable conversations.

[4] For an account of common sense as a 'cultural system', see Geertz 1983. For an account of how common sense diverged from the common sense of Aristotle, see Heller-Roazen 2008.

[5] In a pack of Zener cards, each of the cards displays one of five symbols. Subjects are asked to predict the order of all twenty-five cards when spread before them on a desk. If a subject defies the law of averages by consistently guessing more than five cards correctly, this is taken as evidence of 'psychic ability'.

interoceptive, the spiritual (again) and the psychic senses. Even the neurobiological model of the ten or twenty-one or thirty-three senses must be seen as contingent on the notions of the day. But there is more. In the preceding account, our focus has been on the sensorium as a whole. An equally interesting history could be told of numerous other piecemeal transgressions to the five-sense model, such as the contested notion of speech as a sense (Classen [1993a] 2023: 2; Mazzia 2005); or Jacobson's organ (Watson 1999), which is allegedly responsible for detecting pheromones (sub-olfactory chemical signals); or the genitals as sense organs (Ehm et al. 1999; see further Eschenbaum 2020: 124–6 on titillation).

All of the above-mentioned (and other) candidates for the status of a sixth sense, seventh sense, eighth sense and so on suggest that 'the bounds of sense', such as the philosopher Immanuel Kant understood there to be, are far more variable than he ever imagined. Kant ([1781] 1998) proposed that 'the mind makes the object', and that it does so within the framework of the a priori categories of time and space. We would turn his philosophy on its head. The senses make the object – and the mind, for that matter.

Cultural Variations

When we look across cultures we find that the five-sense model appears to enjoy a certain currency, at least on first impression. For example, in the philosophical texts of the China of the Warring States period (475–221 BCE), the standard model of the sensorium depicted the five senses as five 'officials' with the 'heartmind' (*xin*) as their ruler:

> 'Ear, eye, nose, mouth, and form, each has its own contacts [literally, "receptions" or "meetings"] and does not do things for the others. Now, these are called the heavenly officials. The heartmind dwells in the central cavity and governs the five officials. Now this is called the heavenly ruler' (*Xunzi* quoted in Geaney 2002: 19; see further Blake 2019).

There is a parallel between this notion of the 'heartmind' and 'the common sense' of Aristotle. Incidentally, Aristotle also located the mind (or, rather, the soul) in the heart, rather than the brain.

Probing further, we find that, much as in classical Greece, the ancient Chinese cosmos was a 'sensory cosmology' (Classen [1993a] 2023, 1998). The universe was understood to be composed of five elements (Metal, Wood, Water, Fire and Earth), the human body of five major organs (heart, liver, spleen, kidneys, lungs), the year of five seasons and space of five directions. To these divisions there corresponded five musical tones, five flavours, five colours and so forth. Thus, the element of Fire was associated with a smoky scent, a bitter taste, a red colour, the musical tone *chih*, the season of summer and the direction of South. The element of Water was associated with a rotten smell, a salt taste, the colour black, the musical tone *yu*, the winter season and the direction North (Meade and Emch 2010: 436; Jütte 2005: 25–31).

This elaborate system of correspondences or 'crossmodal connections' (Howes 2023: 188) provided the underpinning for numerous domains of life, from medicine (see Farquhar 2002, 2020) to the ceremonial life of the Emperor and his court. For example, one manual of court etiquette prescribed that, in the first month of spring, 'The Son of Heaven shall live in the apartment to the left of the Green Bright Hall. He shall ride in a belled chariot driven by dark green dragons [horses] and bearing green flags. He shall wear green clothes with green jade. He shall eat wheat and mutton' (cited by Henderson 1984: 53). It bears underlining that, due to the presumed interdependence of all these macrocosmic and microcosmic divisions (they were actually regarded as 'phases' and perhaps 'forces' would be the most apt term to describe them), action in one domain could affect the balance in all the others, setting off a concatenation of changes, but always tending (ideally) to the recovery of equilibrium.

A fivefold schema also informed traditional Indian cosmology:

> The five elements are associated with the five senses, and act as the gross medium for the experience of sensations. The basest element, earth, created using all the other elements, can be perceived by all five senses – (i) hearing, (ii) touch, (iii) sight, (iv) taste, and (v) smell. The next higher element, water, has no odor but can be heard, felt, seen and tasted. Next comes fire, which can be heard, felt and seen. Air can be heard and felt. 'Akasha' (aether) is beyond the senses of smell, taste, sight and touch; it being accessible to the sense of hearing alone.[6]

What is interesting about these alternative models is that they all attest to the link between sensory anatomy and cosmology, and that they all point to the five senses plus one. In other Asian traditions, such as Buddhism, for example, the mind is regarded as a sixth sense. 'In this conception, the mind as a sense organ has as its objects the appearance of any phenomena that do not have material contact as a condition of their immediate possibility: in other words, inner picturing, monologue, intentions, thoughts' (Klima 2002: 201). On this account, the mind is not positioned on a superior plane to the body and the senses, as in the West; rather, it is on a par with them, a sense like any other.

Further explorations reveal ever more variation to the enumeration of the senses across cultures. For example, the Hausa of Nigeria entertain a two-sense

---

[6] This account of Indian sensology and cosmology, which comes from Wikipedia (https://en .wikipedia.org/wiki/Classical_element), finds support in Sarukkai (2014) but requires further substantiation.

model: they have one word for sight (*gani*) and another for hearing, smelling, tasting and touching, understanding, and emotional feeling (*ji*), 'as if all these functions formed part of a single whole' (Ritchie 1991: 194). The Cashinahua of Peru have a six-sense model: they regard the skin, hands, genitals, liver, eyes and ears as 'percipient centres', each with its own kind of knowledge. When asked by an ethnographer 'Does the brain have knowledge?', they responded: '*Hamaki* (it doesn't), … the whole body knows' (Howes 2018: 229–30 and n. 6).

How are we to make sense of this astounding multiplicity of models? I suggest that, rather than simply 'counting', we focus on sensory practices or 'techniques' (including technology) instead. This whole Element is, in fact, about techniques or 'ways of sensing' and the 'worlds of sense' (Classen [1993a] 2023) which they support.

By way of introduction to the notion of 'technique', take the example of the capacity of some blind people to navigate a street or room strewn with obstacles. In the *Blindenpsychologie* of the nineteenth century, this capacity was explained by reference to 'facial vision', a capacity so mysterious that it was dubbed a 'sixth sense'. As Robert Stock (2023) reports, this apparent mystery was pierced as a result of a series of experiments conducted in the psychology laboratory at Cornell University during the 1940s. These experiments involving researchers with visual disabilities (who brought their personal experience to bear on the research question) led to the reconceptualization of 'the sixth sense of the blind' as a matter of technique – the 'audile technique' of perceiving reflected sound, or 'spatial hearing' (also known as echolocation). What is more, the Cornell researchers found that sighted people could learn this technique just as well, if they only tried – that is, if they put their ears to it.

Derivation of 'Sensorium'

We have been using the term 'sensorium' throughout the previous account. A few words are in order about its derivation because its recuperation has played such a vital role in sparking the 'sensorial revolution' in the humanities and social sciences (Howes 2022a). In the early modern period, it referred to 'the seat of sensation in the brain', and it still carries this sense today. However, it also extended to include the circumference of perception. This is apparent in one usage reported in the *Oxford English Dictionary* from 1714: 'The noblest and most exalted Way of considering this infinite Space [referring to "the Universe"] is that of Sir Isaac Newton, who calls it the *Sensorium* of the Godhead'; and in another from 1861: 'Rome became the common sensorium of Europe, and through Rome all the several portions of Latin Europe sympathized and felt with each other.'

This larger social and cosmological sense of the word 'sensorium' has been submerged and practically obliterated under the weight of nineteenth-century psychophysics, augmented further by the authority of contemporary cognitive neuroscience. The reduction of perception to 'patterns of brain activity', as revealed by advances in neuroimaging, has resulted in the retraction of 'sensory processing' from the interface between sense organ and world to the neural pathways that lead from receptor cells to their terminus in the visual cortex, the auditory cortex, the somatosensory cortex and so on (Howes 2022a: 73–5; DeSalle 2018).

The media theorist Walter J. Ong, who was a student of Marshall McLuhan, countered this trend by recuperating the original meaning of the term 'sensorium' in a section of *The Presence of the Word* (Ong 1967). This section was subsequently retrieved and reprinted as the first chapter in *The Varieties of Sensory Experience* (Howes 1991). 'By the sensorium', he writes, 'we mean . . . the entire sensory apparatus as an operational complex', and 'differences in cultures . . . can be thought of as differences in the sensorium, the organization of which is in part determined by culture while at the same time it makes culture' (Ong 1991: 28). The sensory apparatus, according to Ong, includes communication technologies conceived as 'extensions of the senses', following McLuhan (1962). The dominant medium of communication in so-called oral societies is speech; in literate societies, it is writing followed by print; and in contemporary society it is electronic media. These technologies have a strong influence over the organization of mind and society, according to McLuhan and Ong's media theory (Howes and Classen 2013: 70–1, 89–92).

Ong could be said to have 'outered', as McLuhan (1964) would put it, the understanding of how the senses function by directing attention to how they are socialized and technologized, and away from where they are localized in the brain. In effect, the senses are our first media.

This novel observation is pregnant with implications. First, it leads us to think of perception as a public or social activity and not as something which goes on 'in some secret grotto in the head' (Geertz 2001: 76). Second, it shifts the onus from physiology to cultural practice – the sensorium as 'operational complex'. Third, it invites us to conceptualize the sensorium more holistically – that is, as a dynamic whole rather than consisting of so many parts or independent channels. Fourth, and this point is particularly key, it directs our attention to the relations *among* the senses (however many there may be) and to the relations *between* their deliverances (i.e., particular sensations).

This last redirection of attention dovetails with recent advances in experimental psychology and cognitive neuroscience. This body of research points to the significance of the 'multisensory organization' of the brain, 'crossmodal correspondences' and 'sensory interaction' in place of isolation (see generally DeSalle 2018; O'Callaghan 2019; Velasco and Obrist 2020; Howes 2022a: 88–9, 97–8). One of the leading theorists of this area is Charles Spence, Professor of Experimental Psychology and Head of the Crossmodal Research Laboratory at Oxford University. As Gemma Calvert, Spence and Barry E. Stein observe in their introduction to the first edition of *The Handbook of Multisensory Processes*,

> even those experiences that at first may appear to be modality-specific are most likely to have been influenced by activity in other sensory modalities, despite our lack of awareness of such interactions . . . [To] fully appreciate the processes underlying much of sensory perception, we must understand not only how information from each sensory modality is transduced and decoded along the pathways primarily devoted to that sense, but also how this information is modulated by what is going on in the other sensory pathways. (Calvert et al. 2004: xi–xii)

The holistic definition of the sensorium proposed by Ong together with the sensory interaction paradigm advanced by crossmodal researchers like Spence inform the discussion of 'sensory processing' in the sections that follow. Only we diverge from the latter by forsaking the psychology laboratory and taking up the analysis of the senses 'in the open', as it were – that is, in everyday life (Seremetakis 1994, 2019; see further Lévi-Strauss 2020). Our focus shall be on how the senses are constructed and lived differently in different historical periods as well as across cultures – that is, on how the senses are *trained*, which is to say: socialized, enculturated, managed and subjectivized.

Perception as a Matter of Technique

The impetus for this Element came from my reaction to reading *How to Use Your Eyes* (2008) by Professor James Elkins of the School of the Art Institute of Chicago. Elkins' treatise consists of thirty-two chapters dedicated to instructing us 'how to look' at aspects of the physical world ranging from postage stamps to sunsets. 'For me', he writes,

> looking is a kind of pure pleasure – it takes me out of myself and lets me think only of what I am seeing. Also, there is a pleasure in discovering these things [i.e., the sunsets, stamps and so forth]. It is good to know that the visual world is more than television, movies, and art museums, and it is especially good to know that the world is full of fascinating things that can be seen at leisure,

when you are by yourself and there is nothing to distract you. Seeing is, after all, a soundless activity. *It isn't talking, or listening, or smelling, or touching.* It happens best in solitude, when there is nothing in the world but you and the object of your attention. (Elkins 2008: xiii, emphasis added)

This passage struck me as expressing a very limited and, indeed, privileged vision. Why should the other senses be shunted to one side? What about all the ways in which sensory practices, including looking, are shaped by culture? Do people living in situations of poverty or crisis have the time or inclination to gaze at postage stamps? Elkins frames 'looking' as a purely personal or subjective process. He shows little or no awareness of how our perception of the world is informed by social values and mediated by particular techniques and technologies. He even prides himself on turning his back on television, movies and art museums. That is a singularly provincial and uncultured way to use one's eyes, from the sensory studies perspective advanced in this Element.

Consider such devices as the microscope or such media as the movies. It is apparent that these technological media *mediate* – which is to say, modulate – perception. But even before the development of technologies that 'extend the senses' (McLuhan 1962, 1964), there are 'techniques of the senses' (Howes 1990). In his classic essay on 'Techniques of the Body', the anthropologist Marcel Mauss ([1936] 1979: 97) explained that by 'techniques' is meant 'the ways in which from society to society [people] know how to use their bodies'. Mauss went on to list a series of examples of different cultural styles of walking, running, marching, swimming, dancing, jumping, throwing, digging and even sleeping (e.g., dozing while riding a horse, or the use of wooden headrests in Africa), and concluded that 'there is perhaps no "natural way" for the adult' to perform any of these actions: the body is our 'first and most natural instrument'(Mauss ([1936] 1979: 104).

Mauss might have gone on to adduce evidence of cultural differences in the ways of seeing, hearing, touching and so on, but he stopped short. The German sociologist Georg Simmel was alert to this phenomenon, though. In 'Sociology of the Senses', he surmised: 'That [the reason] we get involved in interactions at all depends on the fact that we have a sensory effect upon one another' (Simmel [1907, first English trans. 1921] 1997: 110). Thus, social intercourse is always prompted and modulated by sensory intercourse. By way of illustration, Simmel pointed to how his contemporaries adopted what he called 'the blasé attitude' (*Blasiertheit*) to cope with the barrage of sensations typical of life in the modern metropolis (i.e., filtering sense impressions by creating 'intellectual' distance), how smell was invoked to police social boundaries, and the differing social and cognitive styles of blind people and deaf people.

The insights of Mauss and Simmel into the techniques of the body and the senses lay fallow for much of the twentieth century, at least in English-speaking academia. They had to await the 'sensory turn' of the early 1990s to be retrieved and worked into a general (historical, anthropological and sociological) theory of the 'ways of sensing' (Howes 1990; Classen 1997, 2001; Vannini et al. 2012). This Element seeks to further that agenda. It is about the cultural mediation of perception and the social life of sensation and how these shape – or 'histori-cize' – our cognition and aesthetics. To accomplish this, *Sensorium* onboards the conception of' 'experience' advanced by Caroline A. Jones, Rebecca Uchill and David Mather in their preface to *Experience: Culture, Cognition and the Common Sense*:

> Experience is perpetually on the move. . . . The concept of experience as well as the visceral term anchoring it, have resonant force – calling up complex formulations of individual psychology, life history, the sensorial spectrum, societal norms, technological filtering, and shifting historical epistemes. . . . [I]t also indicates a central problematic: If we can only know reality through our experience, how should we understand the production of experience itself? (Jones et al. 2016: 8; see further Boddice and Smith 2020)

In crafting this Element as a collection of sensory case studies (or *études sensorielles*) responding to this question, my aim is to 'engage familiar and abstruse concepts of experience as specifically material endeavours, in history and at present' (Jones et al. 2016: 8). *Sensorium* thus plunges us into the varieties of sensory experience in history and across cultures. It is particularly attuned to the ways in which the senses interact.

Oh, and the answer to the question with which we began this section – namely, how many senses are there, really? – is that technically – or, to put a finer point on it, 'technique-fully' – considered, the senses are innumerable.[7]

2 Acoustemology: Techniques of Hearing

Acoustemology: A sonic way of knowing and being in the world.
—Steven Feld

In the book *Techniques of Hearing*, edited by Michael Schillmeier, Robert Stock and Beate Ochsner, the notion of techniques of perception (touched on in Section 1) is raised to a new level. Citing the sociologist Georg Simmel, the editors state: 'Our sensory practices allow for specific *techniques of living . . .* techniques of interacting and socializing with others, techniques of engaging

---

[7] The archaeologist Yannis Hamilakis (2014: 5–9) makes a particularly forceful case for the proposition that the senses are 'infinite and innumerable' in *Archaeology and the Senses* (see further Howes 2020).

with our environment (and vice versa), techniques that unfold different processes and modes of societal orderings and transformations' (Schillmeier et al. 2023: 1).

Of particular note is the way *Techniques of Hearing*, being a volume in the Routledge Studies in the Sociology of Health and Illness series, makes a case for expanding the conventional definition of health to include *sensory well-being*. Apart from that, this volume foregrounds the notion of the *interplay* of the senses and the *interface* of senses and technologies. This new focus on *intersensorial* and *intermedia* relations puts paid to the idea of the 'prereflective unity of the senses' and the 'synergic system' of the body that comes out of phenomenology (Merleau-Ponty 1962; Ingold 2000). It does so by highlighting the sociality of sensation and the cultural as well as technological contingency of perceptual processes. On this account, the differential and/or centripetal dynamics of the sensorium are no less worthy of investigation than the centrifugal or so-called synaesthetic – contrary to Merleau-Ponty.[8]

How technical – or, better, 'technique-ful' – is the act of hearing? Not very if you approach it phenomenologically. But to a musician like Pauline Oliveros (2005) with her practice of 'deep listening',[9] to the blind theologian and educator John M. Hull (1992) with his notion of 'whole-body seeing', or to an anthropologist like Steven Feld (2005) who coined the term 'acoustemology' to describe the 'sensuous epistemology' of the Kaluli people of Papua New Guinea (whose social and ceremonial life is informed by the acoustic motif of 'lift-up-over-sounding'), *the technicity of hearing is everything*. It is only because our normal ways of hearing get internalized, become habitual and therefore 'sink' to the level of the subconscious (Bateson 1972) that they seem 'natural'.

There is a marked unevenness to the treatment of the senses in the sensory studies literature. Far more attention has been devoted to seeing ('visual culture') than to hearing, and to hearing than to touch, and so on. This can be attributed to the enduring influence of the traditional Western hierarchy of the senses on our thinking about perception: vision is 'the noblest sense', the most

---

[8] Merleau-Ponty (1962: 235, 229) writes: 'my body is a ready-made system of equivalents and transpositions from one sense to another. The senses translate each other without any need of an interpreter, and are mutually comprehensible without the intervention of any idea. ... Synaesthetic perception is the rule.' This is a truncated view. The senses stand in many other relations to each other than just 'translation' – relations such as domination, discord, complementarity, assistance (or cooperation), anticipation and sequencing (see Howes 2022a: 26–7). All of these examples involve the modulation of one sense by another, rather than 'equivalence' *tout court*.

[9] 'Walk so silently that the bottoms of your feet become ears' (Oliveros quoted in Bath et al. 2023: 140).

'informative', et cetera; hearing is 'the second sense'; touch is 'the lowest sense'; and so forth. If 'the time of the senses' is now, though, as Regina Bendix (2005) avers, then it is time to extirpate these prejudices and 'rebalance' the senses (Spence 2021); it is time to entertain the idea of a heterarchical sensorium and explore other combinations apart from the audiovisual (Howes 2022a: 12).

Echolocation is one example of a technique of hearing. As will be recalled from the discussion of this technique in Section 1, during the nineteenth century the ability of certain blind persons to navigate a room strewn with obstacles was construed as a mysterious 'sixth sense' ('facial vision'). Then, in the mid twentieth century, research carried out at Cornell University led to the discovery that this capacity is actually a matter of technique – the 'audile technique' of perceiving reflected sound, or 'spatial hearing' (Stock 2023). In 'Hearing like an animal: Exploring acoustic experience beyond human ears', Judith Willkomm and Asher Boersma (2023) take us further afield. Their chapter discusses breaking research in the field of bioacoustics that uses sonic devices to investigate the auditory worlds of non-human animals. It emerges that enabling humans to 'hear like an animal' involves researchers imagining, then learning, through an interplay of senses and technology, about non-human acoustic experience. Departing from the conventional focus on bird songs, Willkomm and Boersma (2023) discuss 'hearing like a dog' and 'singing like a bat', before delving into 'hearing underwater'.

> It is difficult to observe acoustic communication between animals under water because researchers cannot share this acoustic space permanently and are confronted with different hearing conditions than on land. Therefore, the history of marine bioacoustics is deeply entangled with media technologies that helped to explore, to surveil, and to control the oceanic territory acoustically ... Famously, the first recordings of whale songs were made by hydrophones, but were considered by the US navy as a disruptive by-product of the monitoring of the ocean for enemy submarines. (Willkomm and Boersma 2023: 131)

This military research led to the development of sonar technology, which was modelled after cetaceous modes of navigation and communication (Connor 2006). Perversely, the application of this same technology by the US and other navies has had a horrendously disruptive impact on cetacean communicative and affective life (Shiga 2017). Willkomm and Boersma (2023) express the hope that hearing in the expanded field will inspire humanity to empathize with sea creatures, and come to treat them as fellow sentient beings – and it has to some degree, but not sufficiently to displace the perception of cetaceous species as 'resources' to be 'harvested', or as expendable in the interests of 'national security'.[10]

There are evidently frictions between technique and technology, which occur both at the interface of human and natural worlds and within human society itself. In 'Listening or reading? Rethinking ableism in relation to the senses and (acoustic) text' (Schulz 2023), the blind sociologist Miklas Schulz explores the tension between the faculty of audition and its technological extensions by means of talking books, reader screens and other devices for use by people with low vision. Schulz employs interviews with sighted and visually impaired individuals and autoethnography to examine reading every which way (seeing text, hearing text, speaking internally), assisted and unassisted, for work or for entertainment. His chapter offers a stunning critique of ableist assumptions concerning reading, as well as his own theory of how the conflict of the modalities involved in reading could be resolved. Here, again, it is the idea of the interplay among the faculties and between the faculties and technology that is foregrounded and that proves most illuminating for what it tells us about hetero-aesthesia in place of synaesthesia.[11]

In his chapter, Markus Spöhrer (2023) explores how a video game in which vision is sidelined in favour of hearing can transform one's experience of space. The game in question, called *A Blind Legend*, leads the gamer by the ears: binaural auditory cues enable players to detect the location and interact with virtual characters and objects in the imaginary space of the game. This game is not only eyes-free; it also liberates the gamer from having to remain seated in front of a computer screen: space becomes a direction in motion rather than a static container or an a priori category (*pace* Kant [1781] 1998). Spöhrer introduces the notion of 'techno-sensory configuration' to conceptualize the core mechanism of the game: its arrangement enables immersive effects and auditory play to take shape at the conjuncture of human, technological,

---

[10] As will be discussed in Section 5, Margaret Lucas Cavendish was among the first to think and feel across species boundaries. (In this respect, she stood in virulent contrast to René Descartes, who conceived of animals as automatons.) Parenthetically, there is an emerging literature within biology on animal sensing which goes under the name of 'sensory ecology' (e.g., Yong 2020; Stevens 2021): it is radically expanding our understanding of and appreciation for the 'sensory exotica' of other species. Anthropologists have also increasingly turned their attention to expanding the practice of ethnography beyond the human, whence 'multispecies ethnography' (Smart and Smart 2017; Fijn and Kavesh 2021; Chao et al. 2022). There is also a growing body of work within sensory history on senses and animal histories (e.g., Smith 2022). Centring animal sensing and human–animal sensory relationships in this way can help dilute the tendency, which is especially prevalent in the Global North (Santos 2018), to see animals as mere resources.

[11] An early example of hetero-aesthesia, or the 'collideroscope' of the sensorium (McLuhan 1962: 75), can be found in Marshall McLuhan's ruminations on a device used in the dentistry of his day known as the Audiac: it involved the use of headphones to 'bombard the patient with enough noise to block pain from the dentist's drill' (Eric McLuhan quoted in Howes 2022a: 128).

discursive and sensory configurations and related bodily techniques of hearing and tactile navigation. *A Blind Legend* is, therefore, an audio-tactile game which offers an exhilarating alternative to the hegemony of the audiovisual in our ludic life.[12]

The issue of how sensory practices are transformed by sensory technologies is one of far-reaching relevance. For example, in his examination of the emergent use of sound-masking technology in the office environments of the 1970s (when 'white noise' was used to recondition acoustic space), Joeri Bruyninckx (2023) exposes how this development resulted in a particular idealization of hearing and working (tied to considerations of efficiency and productivity) coming to be encoded in the technology. This, Bruyninckx avers, should compel us to reflect critically on 'the politics of "smart" hearing'. In 'The future is ear', Beate Ochsner and Shintaro Miyazaki (2023) explore 'smart hearing' further by highlighting the *contradictions* that this techno-mediated practice smuggles in. They ask: 'What are the effects and implications of "smart" hearing technologies which offer new functionalities that promise ever-better hearing, fitness and well-being while, at the same time, shifting responsibilities to the hearing subjects?' (Ochsner and Mitazaki 2023: 92). The new normal responsibilizes individuals to upgrade their hearing so they become fully functional citizens, with the result that they get caught up in 'neo-liberal circuits of consumerism and techno-capitalism' (Ochsner and Mitazaki 2023: 92).

The market for assistive hearables (as 'lifestyle products') has, indeed, expanded exponentially in recent years, but questions arise concerning the commercialization and the standardization of the sense of hearing that this entails. Does the new calibration not spell a loss of hearing diversity, or foster an auditory class divide between those who can afford to enhance their hearing and those who cannot? We can already see the multiple controversies and divides resulting from the use of cochlear implants to treat hearing loss, with high-income individuals and countries more likely to have access to such implants than low-income individuals and countries, and deaf communities concerned about pressures to mainstream deaf children into the hearing world

---

[12] Might the invention of this audio-tactile game open the way for the creation of audio-olfactory or audio-gustatory games? There are precedents. One thinks of the figure of Des Esseintes in J.-K. Huysmans' ([1884] 1959) *Against Nature* playing 'internal symphonies' with his 'mouth organ', which consisted of a selection of liqueurs that correspond to different musical sounds (Classen 1998: 115). The example of *kōdō*, the Japanese incense ceremony, also comes to mind (to be discussed in Section 3). All that prevents these highly palatable and aromatic alternatives from being entertained and developed is the fetishization of the audiovisual in our 'Video-Christian civilization' (de Kerckhove 1998). Most videogame consoles have no smell- or taste-track, and those which do are woefully rudimentary.

through a technological transformation (Fagan and Tarabichi 2018; Friedner 2022).

To return to the subject of spatial hearing, as brought out in Robert Stock's (2023) chapter on echolocation and Spöhrer's (2023) autoethnography of playing *A Blind Legend*, Jens Gerrit Papenberg (2023) also addresses this phenomenon. Hearing was long considered a purely temporal sense (it takes time to hear a sentence or listen to a piece of music) in contrast to vision (the eyes can take in a scene all at once), and sound was understood in terms of such parameters as 'frequency' and 'pitch'. As Papenberg relates, developments in loudspeaker and other audio technologies in 1930s Germany challenged the prevailing conception and led to the redefinition of sound as a 'voluminous entity', hence as having extension in space. The 'fuzziness' of the emergent conception of sound volume may be attributed to the way it transgresses or blurs the so-called a priori categories (Kant [1781] 1998) of time and space, hearing and seeing.

The digitization, or technological augmentation, of sound and hearing has the potential to enhance social interaction and social well-being. However, while 'sonic self-care' through the use of hearables (Rennies 2023) and the proliferation of 'adaptive generated soundscapes' produced by programs like the ambient-sound app Endel (Haffke 2023)[13] hold out the promise of self-determination and 'hearing 4 all', they do so only within the framework of cyber-consumer capitalism. Thus, 'self-empowerment' comes at a price in terms of affordability, personal autonomy (due to the need to rely on experts to get oneself fitted with a device) and privacy. Can the neo-liberal capitalist circuits be broken? Ochsner and Miyazaki (2023) argue in favour of de-medicalizing the definition and treatment of hearing impairment and technicizing it instead by means of hearables. They also propose countering the monopolization of user data by big corporations (with their proprietary codes) by open-sourcing it (e.g., OpenMHA, LoCHAId), and allowing self-fitting, self-adjusting (or do-it-yourself) communities of assisted hearers to flourish.

The difficulty is that these proposals all rely on the technologization of hearing and overlook or belie the very title of the book: *Techniques of Hearing*. Of course, communications engineers and audiologists (especially) will remain fixated on technological 'solutions' without paying due attention to the sociality of communication (Lloyd and Tremblay 2021). What is doubly

---

[13] So too with the technology of 'mobile music listening' (listening to music over headphones in public), beginning with the Sony Walkman and continuing with the iPod (Bull 2000, 2007), which blocks out the din of the metropolis and can serve as 'an accompaniment for the lonely' (Schurig 2023: 70). But we should not lose track of the social deprivation that this privatization of listening entails. Significantly, the inventor of the Walkman, Akio Morita, designed it to have two jacks because enjoying music privately was inconceivable to him.

troubling, though, is that these specialists completely ignore the many rich and varied ways in which the use of the 'unaided' senses can be enhanced, as documented by musicians and anthropologists. For example, there is the *Bodily Listening in Place* research-creation project led by Ellen Waterman (director of the Research Centre for Music, Sound and Society at Carleton University) in collaboration with Tiphanie Girault (a deaf artist, communicating and directing in sign language) and Paula Bath (a PhD candidate in anthropology at Concordia University), co-founders of sPiLL.PROpagation, an artist centre for creation and production in sign language in Canada. Their project explored 'processes of intersensory and intercultural exchange across hearing and deaf experience, and through sonic, haptic, kinetic, linguistic, and graphic media'; it culminated in the production of 'an instructional score for intersensory improvisation' (Bath et al. 2023: 139).

Casting the net wider, there is Peter Graif's (2018) *Being and Hearing: Making Intelligible Worlds in Deaf Kathmandu*, an ethnography of hearing and deafness in Nepal which centres on the idiosyncratic jottings and sign language of a cognitively impaired but highly astute deaf youth. There is Michele Friedner's (2022) *Sensory Futures: Deafness and Cochlear Implant Infrastructures in India*. There is Anthony Seeger's ([1988] 2004) *Why Suyá Sing*, a 'musical anthropology' of an Amazonian people, and Ellen Basso's (1985) *A Musical View of the Universe: Kalapalo Myth and Ritual Performances*, which concerns the acoustic world of the Kalapalo. And there is the tremendously inspiring acoustic *oeuvre* of Steven Feld, beginning with *Sound and Sentiment: Birds, Weeping, Poetics and Song in Kaluli Expression* (Feld [1982] 2012) and continuing with 'Voices of the Rainforest' (Feld 1991b; see further Feld and Boudreault-Fournier 2022). The Kaluli people of Papua New Guinea with whom Feld worked are accomplished aurators. For example, they taught him how to hear the 'inside' of a drumbeat (Feld 1991a). The techniques of hearing, or 'acoustemologies', documented in these ethnographic studies could be a source of great instruction for communication engineers and audiologists based in the Global North, if they would but heed them.

3 Osmology: Ways of Smelling

Osmology: The study of the nature and social roles of odour.

—Constance Classen

The exhibition *Belle Haleine: The Scent of Art*, which ran from February to May 2015 at the Museum Tinguely in Basel, represented a turning point in the history of aesthetics. I was reminded, as I prepared a paper for an interdisciplinary symposium held in conjunction with the show, of another such exhibition three years prior, when the New York Museum of Arts and

Design put on *The Art of Scent, 1889–2012*, curated by Chandler Burr. The latter exhibition's stated objective was to 'situate olfactory art within the larger historical context of the visual arts'. Burr accordingly assembled twelve perfumes, from *Jicky* by Aimé Guerlain to *Angel* by Olivier Cresp and *Osmanthe Yunnan* by Jean-Claude Ellena, in a bid to put perfumery on a par with painting.

A colleague of mine who visited the Chandler Burr show was not, however, impressed. 'How sweet', she commented when talking to me about it, echoing that line in *The Foul and the Fragrant* (1986) where Alain Corbin writes of the nineteenth-century French bourgeoisie seizing control of the sense of smell and constructing 'a schema of perception based on the pre-eminence of sweetness' (Corbin 1986: 141). *The Art of Scent* exhibition was indeed very 'sweet'. It did not include any scents that pushed the envelope, none of the compositions of, for example, the renowned Norwegian smell artist Sissel Tolaas. By contrast, Tolaas' installation *The Smell of Fear – The Fear of Smell* (2006–15) figured as one of the centrepieces of *The Scent of Art* at the Tinguely. For this piece, Tolaas captured the sweat of twenty paranoiac men during periods of crisis and incorporated its odour in little patches on the walls of the 10 x 10 metre room where the installation was housed, with each subject's smell identified by a number. To experience the individual smells, the visitor had to scratch the walls, but there was also a composite odour that suffused the atmosphere with a distinct edge.

The exclusion of Tolaas' work from *The Art of Scent* exhibition raises interesting questions concerning its status as art. Can a work such as *The Smell of Fear – The Fear of Smell* be considered aesthetic when it inspires uncomfortable sensations, when it is in no way 'sweet'? I would argue that, while Tolaas' installation may not be very pleasing, it is aesthetic, like a number of the other works by avant-garde artists that surrounded it at *The Scent of Art* exhibition. These ranged from Marcel Duchamp's *Air de Paris* (1919) to Carsten Höller's pheromone-breathing scent machine, *Hypothèse de grue* (2013).

Avant-garde artists have, of course, been shocking the senses of the bourgeoisie from the start (Classen 2014c; Higgins 2014). But were it not for their efforts the art world would have remained stuck in a rut. We should be thankful to them for their dogged determination to extend the bounds of the aesthetic. What is not so commonly recognized, however, is that, in doing so, they have also been reclaiming something of the original meaning of the term 'aesthetic'. In other words, there is a retro aspect to their forwardness.

The term 'aesthetic' was coined by the eighteenth-century German philosopher Alexander von Baumgarten. He took it over from the Greek *aestheta*, which refers to things perceived by the senses as distinct from *noeta*, or that which can be known intellectually, through logic, like the truths of mathematics. 'Baumgarten was determined to raise *aestheta* to a science with its own rules and truths, which might be comparable to the rules and truths of logic, although not as clear' (Allen 2008: n.p.).[14] To this end, he held that the aesthetic is rooted in the body and the senses – that is, in perception rather than the intellect – and that beauty is in the senses of the beholder, rather than an inherent quality of the art object. To put this another way, the aesthetic has to do primarily with the perfection of perception, and only secondarily with the perception of perfection, or 'beauty'. Properly understood, then, the aesthetic is a way of sensing that involves grasping what Baumgarten called 'the unity-in-multiplicity of sensible qualities' (quoted in Gregor 1983: 370).

Unfortunately, Baumgarten's sensuously minded definition quickly got tidied up (purified of 'confusion') and objectified by Immanuel Kant. For Kant, as for his legions of followers, aesthetics proper involves the 'disinterested contemplation' of some art object and should result in the passing of a judgment that is, in principle, free and universalizable. This redefinition not only paved the way for the bourgeoisification of 'taste' (in the metaphorical sense), as Pierre Bourdieu (1984) has shown in his social critique of the judgment of taste, but also opened the way for the disqualification of smell. 'To what organic sense do we owe the least and which seems to be the most dispensable?' Kant asked, then replied:

> 'The sense of smell. It does not pay us to cultivate it or to refine it in order to gain enjoyment; this sense can pick up more objects of aversion than of pleasure (especially in crowded places) and, besides, the pleasure coming from the sense of smell cannot be other than fleeting and transitory' (Kant 1978: 46).

Kant's disqualification was the first blow against smell, not just as an aesthetic sense but also as a cognitive sense. This prejudice has persisted. For example, in *Visual Thinking*, the art psychologist Rudolf Arnheim (1969: 19) wrote: 'one can indulge in smells and tastes, but one can hardly think in them'. This is in contrast to the senses of sight and hearing. The aesthetic and cognitive or 'intellectual' vocation of these senses has long been treated as given in the Western tradition. The curious thing is that smell was also seen as an intellectual sense in premodernity. For example, 'nose-wise' (now obsolete) could mean either 'clever' or 'keen-scented', and the words 'sagacious' and 'sage' derive

---

[14] Why 'not as clear'? Because the truths of, for example, mathematics are self-evident (logical), whereas the evidence of the senses is always suspect, 'confused and indistinct' by comparison, according to a long-standing prejudice that was expressed most forcefully by Descartes.

from Latin words meaning 'to have a good sense of smell' (Classen [1993a] 2023: ch. 3). Moreover, on account of its identification with the breath (Latin *spiritus*), smell was widely understood to be the most spiritual of the senses (Classen 1998: ch. 2). Thus, Kant broke with these traditions by summarily dismissing the cognitive and the spiritual value of smell.

The second strike against smell was levelled by Sigmund Freud. In a lengthy footnote to *Civilization and Its Discontents* (Freud 1953–74, vol. 21), Freud made much of the 'diminution of olfactory stimuli' that supposedly resulted from our forebears assuming an upright posture. No longer would we humans go about on all fours, like dogs, sniffing everything in our path. However, the population of the premodern West, unaware of the fact that they had been deprived of their sense of smell by the march of evolution, derived rich meaning from the odours around them. The French historian Lucien Febvre ([1942] 1982: 432) noted in this regard that the 'sixteenth century did not see first: it heard and smelled'. Sight revealed nothing beyond surfaces, while smell accessed the essence of things (see Classen et al. 1994). When Freud dismissed smell as an outmoded sense in humans, far from declaring an 'evolutionary fact', he was simply chiming in with the culturally anosmic tune of the time (Corbin 1986).

The third strike against smell in modernity was delivered by the writer who, paradoxically, is commonly considered its greatest champion, Marcel Proust. In his novel *À la recherche du temps perdu* (1913–27), Proust famously described how the sensations of eating a madeleine dipped in tea evoked scenes from his youth. This experience of 'total recall' stimulated by a familiar scent or taste is now known as the 'Proust Effect' (van Campen 2014).[15]

While the madeleine incident might seem like a celebration of smell, it was actually a demotion, which compounded the Kantian devaluation of olfaction on cognitive and aesthetic grounds. No good for thinking, at least smell is good for emoting and remembering, the doctrine insinuates. And so smell has come to be known as 'the affective sense', with the result that the gap between it and the intellectual and aesthetic senses of sight and hearing has grown ever wider. This is not to suggest that smell may not be good for stimulating recall or triggering emotions, only that that is not all that smell is good for. By way of example, consider Francis Galton's invention of a smell arithmetic. It employed scents in place of written numerals, but proved effective at facilitating calculations

---

[15] It will be noticed that the Proust Effect was produced by a taste, not a smell. This distinction is commonly disregarded in most discussions of the topic, since smell and taste are both 'chemical senses', and so are regularly taken to be interchangeable, or even one and the same (Mollo et al. 2022). However, these two senses can be elaborated culturally in very different ways. Consider, for example, the fact that 'tasty' is a positive term in English while 'smelly' is a negative term.

(Galton 1894). The idea that mathematical operations could be conducted olfactorily never caught on, though. The Western world had already moved on to what could be called the stage of visualization, where only sight would do for 'higher' cognitive functions.

To arrive at a proper understanding of the aesthetic and cognitive potential of smell we must look outside the Western tradition, to those traditions where it does not carry all the baggage, all the disqualifications, that Kant and Freud and Proust (or Proust's interpreters) have saddled it with. Let us turn to consider how the sense of smell and the art of smell have been elaborated in Indian culture. In what follows, we shall be drawing on James McHugh's (2012) analysis of olfactory culture in *Sandalwood and Carrion*, which focusses on premodern India.

To recap, we have seen how, in the West following Proust, the dominant understanding of smell is as a temporal sense, the sense of recollection. Smell acts inwardly; it bridges time and resonates through the corridors of memory. In India, by contrast, smell is traditionally a spatial sense. It acts outwardly, and is a force for either attraction or repulsion, on the analogy of the way a person is drawn to a flower by its scent, while the smell of carrion is found repellent. As a spatial sense, smell is not primarily concerned with recollection. McHugh is very clear on this: 'In Sanskrit literature, smells are no more prominent than other sensory stimuli when it comes to memory (e.g., in contexts of remembering and longing for absent lovers). ... It is not the case that when smells are present memories are automatically triggered' (McHugh 2012: 14). This observation will come as a surprise to many a psychologist and neuroscientist, but so be it. If they were more sensitive to cultural diversity, they wouldn't make such grand pronouncements regarding 'the nature of smell' or 'the biological function of olfaction' in the first place.

While not privileged in processes of recollection, being a spatial sense, smell is good for navigation. By way of illustration, McHugh points to a scene in a well-known play, *Ratnāvalī*, where a king sniffs his way around the royal pleasure garden on his way to a secret tryst with his mistress in the dead of night: 'This is surely the border of *campakas*; this is that beautiful *sinduvāra*, and this is the dense hedge of *bakula* trees; this is the row of *pātalas*', the King muses. McHugh (2012: 28) explains: 'The path in this place, though concealed by double darkness, becomes clear by means of the signs of the trees recognized by constantly sniffing the varied perfume.' Here, smell has replaced sight (disabled by darkness) as the sense that orients a person in space, and leads them to their destination. This scenario introduces us to a very different way of thinking about the cognitive potential of smell. It is positively geographical.[16]

Indian perfumery practices also disrupt deep-seated assumptions. In the West, perfume is normally applied in the form of a textureless, mildly tinted liquid. Perfumery is basically a unimodal art. In India, perfume normally takes the form of a paste, and has a plethora of sensible qualities. Consider the following description of *candana* (sandalwood): 'Light, unctuous, not dry, smearing oil like ghee, of pleasant smell, suitable for the skin, mild, not fading, tolerant of warmth, absorbs great heat, and pleasant to touch – these are the qualities of sandalwood' (quoted in McHugh 2012: 187). Preparations involving sandalwood are thus valued not only for their smell but also for their light white or yellow colour (sight), cooling potency (temperature), pleasing feel (touch) and longevity (other aromatics fade), in addition to being exotic and expensive. This explains their vaunted status alongside gemstones in royal treasuries, their use to cut fever and incite pleasure and for visual body decoration. Perfumery in India is thus a multimodal art. To prepare or appreciate the effects of sandalwood involves grasping 'the unity-in-multiplicity of sensible qualities', as Baumgarten would say.

Another example of this notion of smell as the sense of navigation – that is, a spatial sense that acts outwardly rather than a temporal sense that unfolds inwardly – is given in the Japanese incense ceremony (*kōdō*), particularly the version known as 'The Three Scenic Views' (Miyajima in Hiroshima Prefecture, Amanohashidate in Kyoto Prefecture and Matsushima in Miyagi Prefecture). The idea is that the participants are to imagine themselves on a boat ride to the three famous sites, it being the scent of the different woods used in the rite that transports them to each destination, providing they guess correctly (Howes 2011). The interest of this ceremony lies in the way it uses the medium of smell to help participants visualize spaces, rather than relying on photographs or verbal descriptions. It is a way of developing the olfactory imagination, both the capacity to discriminate smells and the capacity to form associations through scents. There is nothing resembling this form of mind-travel in Western culture, except perhaps for cinema, but then cinema only traffics in visual and acoustic images; it has no smell-track. Little wonder that smell has become the least educated of the senses in the modern West.

By contrast, in Japan people do take an interest in the education of olfaction. There is a 'way of smelling' in the context of *kōdō*. This involves inclining one's head, lifting the censer to one's nose with one hand while cupping the smoke with the other, sniffing three times and then turning one's head to the side so as

---

[16] Likewise, among the Ongee of the Little Andaman Islands, space and time and personhood are all mediated by smell. Their cosmology is a veritable osmology (Classen et al. 1994: ch. 4).

not to disturb the ash in the censer when one breathes out. There is a special quality to the attention shaped by this way of smelling, too. The Japanese refer to it as 'listening to the incense' (*ko wo kiku*). This is to underscore the difference between it and normal, everyday smelling, in the same way that listening differs from (mere) hearing, but note how this usage also imparts a multisensory dimension to the participants' attention.

One final thing to note about the Japanese incense ceremony is that its name, *kōdō*, means 'way of fragrance' – that is, it is a practice, a way (*dao*) or performance art, if you will, rather than an art form, such as painting or perfumery (see further Howes and Classen 2013: ch. 1). *Kōdō* is a practice informed by the ideal of the perfection of perception, which may also involve the perception of perfection. Baumgarten would approve. Kant would just turn up his nose.

We have seen how smell is the sense of space in India and Japan, but it can also function as the sense of time. Consider sixteenth-century China. Prior to the arrival of missionaries from Europe, who introduced the Chinese to mechanical timepieces, the main methods of time reckoning included astronomical and water clocks, while gongs and drums were employed to mark off periods of time within cities. The most prevalent method of telling time in imperial China, however, was the use of incense (Bedini 1994). This penchant is evidenced by the popular expression 'in the time it takes to burn an incense stick'.

Burning incense was a common religious ritual in China and its association with the passage of time may well have led to the development of the incense clock. These incense clocks, which could be simple or very elaborate, measured time in two basic ways. One way was that a passage of time would be indicated by an incense stick of a certain length burning out. Another way was that the fragrance emitted by the incense would change after a certain amount of time. Such incense clocks were used in both homes and temples. This smell-infused understanding of time would have provided a highly engaging experience: time was 'in the air', one 'breathed' it in, and did not simply 'read' it on a clock face. The experience of time, as mediated by the incense clock, was thus qualitative instead of purely quantitative, and immersive rather than objective. The cultural significance of this olfactory way of imagining time was also informed by the way the Chinese regarded the fragrance of incense as an aid to thoughtfulness, a stimulus to conversation and a mental and physical purifier. However, as a result of the Jesuit missionaries introducing the Chinese to mechanical clocks, the scenting of time and the use of smell as an aid to thoughtfulness would gradually recede in importance (see Howes 2023: ch. 7).

This section has tracked the devaluation and dismissal of smell as a spiritual, intellectual and/or aesthetic sense in modern European history. It has also disclosed aspects of the elaboration of smell in diverse Asian cultures – India, China and Japan – and thereby (hopefully) enlarged our sense of what smell is good for. Meanwhile, *Belle Haleine: The Scent of Art* at the Tinguely can be seen as having opened a breach in the web of prejudices that has come to surround smell in the modern period, and thereby contributed to the expansion of aesthetic experience and the recovery of the original meaning of the category of the aesthetic, as envisioned by Baumgarten, before Kant got hold of it. Significantly, the exhibition did so by exposing visitors to a full range of smells, not just the pleasant fragrances of *The Art of Scent* exhibition at the New York Museum of Arts and Design. This enlargement of the smells we think with and turn into art recalls our minds to the olfactory plenitude of the world in which we live.

4 Sensology: How to See Feelingly

Sensology: The transdisciplinary investigation of perception and the human senses in all their facets as embodied cultural constructions.

—Richard Newhauser

According to the seventeenth-century British philosopher John Locke ([1689] 1975), in *An Essay Concerning Human Understanding*, the senses 'receive' impressions of the external world which in turn become 'Ideas'. *Nihil in intellectu quod non prius in sensu*, or 'There can be nothing in the mind that has not first been in the senses'. On this account, the perceiving subject is figured as a patient (not an agent), and the mind is represented as a blank slate (*tabula rasa*) at birth. This empiricist understanding of how the senses function departed from the idealist doctrines of Plato and later Descartes, who held that 'Ideas' (innate ideas) come first, and these are recognized through the senses. On this account, the mind takes precedence over the senses.

In its passivity, or denial of any sort of agency to the senses (or to those doing the sensing), Locke's understanding also departed from another long-standing conception of how the senses work: the extramission theory of vision. This theory held that the eyes emit rays. There is no trace of this theory in Locke's *Essay*; the senses have been pacified and made to retreat inside the head (Howes 2023: ch. 4).[17]

Another key tenet of Locke's understanding was that each sense has its proper sphere: vision has colour, hearing has sound, smell has odour and so on. This modular or piecemeal conception of the sensorium was challenged by an

---

[17] Of course, this understanding survives outside the scientific study of perception, for example in the widespread popular belief in the powers of 'the evil eye', and such expressions as 'looking daggers' and 'the eyes of love'.

anecdote that had been brought to Locke's attention, which he recounted as follows:

> A studious blind man, who had mightily beat his head about visible objects, and made use of the explication of his books and friends, to understand those names of light and colours which often came in his way, bragged one day, That he now understood what scarlet signified. Upon which, his friend demanding what scarlet was? The blind man answered, It was like the sound of a trumpet. (Locke [1689] 1975: ch. 4, para. 11)

How true! the reader may think. But Locke does not cite this anecdote to endorse the blind man's suggestion, only to ridicule it: 'For, to hope to produce an idea of light or colour by a sound, however formed, is to expect that sounds should be visible, or colours audible; and to make the ears do the office of all the other senses. Which is all one as to say, that we might taste, smell, and see by the ears' (Locke [1689] 1975: ch. 4, para. 11). Any suggestion that it could be possible to form ideas in or about one sense by means of another is out of the question for Locke.

The Lockean idea of the senses as passive receptors has been challenged by numerous scholars of perception (Gregory 2015; Noë 2006), but by none more forcefully than the philosopher Michel Serres (2008) in *The Five Senses: A Philosophy of Mingled Bodies*. Writing about the sensory traits of skin, he states:

> our skin is a mixture of [sense organs], like a palette. . . . in it, through it, with it, the world and my body touch each other, the feeling and the felt, it defines their common edge. . . . I do not wish to call the place in which I live a [milieu], I prefer to say that things mingle with each other and that I am no exception to that, I mix with the world which mixes with me. (Serres 2009: 79–80)

On this account, the body is not a discrete entity and the senses 'mingle' both with the world and with each other, just as persons do. This is the first case of what it might mean to 'see feelingly', to be considered in this section.[18]

The 'Collideroscope' of the Sensorium

There is a growing body of research that supports Serres' relational and interactive understanding of how the senses operate. This research departs from the conventional sense-by-sense – or one-sensory-modality-at-a-time – approach to the study of perceptual processes within psychology. Charles

---

[18] The phrase 'to see feelingly' comes from Shakespeare (Dundas 1985). There is also a variation on it in the writings of the American naturalist Henry David Thoreau: 'A man has not seen a thing who has not felt it' (Thoreau 1906, vol. 19: 160).

Spence, Head of the Crossmodal Research Laboratory at Oxford University, is a leading exponent of this new opening of the senses to each other, and to the world. Spence's approach stresses modulation over modularity.

Examples of such modulation culled from everyday experience include the fact that, in noisy surroundings, speakers can be understood more easily if they can be seen as well as heard; and the so-called ventriloquism effect, where the seen lip-movements of the dummy alter or 'capture' the apparent location of the speech sounds – a phenomenon known as 'visual dominance'.

Many of the studies in *The Handbook of Multisensory Processes* (2004) edited by Calvert, Spence and Stein use neuroimaging techniques to pinpoint the multiple sites of multisensory processing in the brain, including many regions long thought to be modality-specific or 'primary sensory' areas, as distinct from the so-called higher order associative areas traditionally assumed to be responsible for the formation of unified percepts out of the diversity of inputs. In addition to demonstrating the functional interdependence of the modalities, a number of these studies point to the functional equivalence or adaptability of the modalities. For example, it is now recognized that sensory-specific areas can be 'recruited' or 'remapped' via other sensory-specific areas in situations of sensory deprivation or intensive perceptual training. Thus, the visual cortex in blind individuals has been found to show activation in auditory tasks, while the auditory cortex in deaf individuals can be activated by visual tasks (Sur 2004; Röder and Rösler 2004). Such evidence of adaptive processing, or 'crossmodal plasticity', underscores the importance of adopting a relational approach to the study of the sensorium in place of assuming that the senses are structurally and functionally distinct.

The possibility of experiencing the content of one sensory modality by means of another was actualized in the context of various experiments with prosthetic devices in the mid twentieth century. These devices included the tactile-visual substitution system (TVSS) invented by Paul Bach-y-Rita. The TVSS is a complex apparatus involving a head-mounted television camera linked to electrically driven vibrators attached to a square of skin on the back of a blind person. The device 'throws' an image of the objects in the blind person's surroundings onto the patch of skin, and this tactile stimulation is transposed into visual information in the brain, thereby enabling the person to move in space without bumping into things (see generally Zika 2018; Paterson 2021; Salter 2022). This is the second case of 'seeing feelingly' to be considered here.

In his research, Spence, in association with diverse co-researchers, has explored and tested a wide variety of combinations among the modalities (see Spence 2018, 2021; Howes 2022a: 84–9, 94–9). Spence envisions the sensorium as a combinatory or a 'collideroscope', to use McLuhan's term in *The*

Gutenberg Galaxy (McLuhan 1962: 75). Mention of McLuhan's name will remind the reader of how his student Walter Ong challenged the assumption that the senses are localized in the receptor organs or reducible to their 'seat' in the brain by recuperating an older definition of 'the sensorium' that highlighted its social and cosmological dimensions. Ong and McLuhan further urged that 'media' (in the expanded sense) be regarded as 'extensions of the senses': clothing as an extension of the skin, the automobile of the foot, the book of the eye, the telephone of the ear (McLuhan and Fiore 1967).

McLuhan and Ong's theory of the senses as media takes us beyond the artificial confines of the psychology laboratory and into the realm of the anthropology and history of the senses – that is, the senses in everyday life (Seremetakis 2019). Attending to the enculturation and the historicity of the senses and cognition is central to the pursuit of 'sensory studies' (Bull et al. 2006). This cross-disciplinary field of inquiry emerged out of the sensory turn in the humanities and the social sciences in the closing decades of the twentieth century, which gave rise to such approaches as the history of the senses and the anthropology of the senses, and such interdisciplinary fields as visual culture, auditory culture (or sound studies) and taste culture, all of which come under the umbrella term 'sensory studies' (Howes 2022a: 4–11).

Constance Classen, in such works as *Worlds of Sense: Exploring the Senses in History and Across Cultures* ([1993a] 2023), *Inca Cosmology and the Human Body* (1993b) and the six-volume *A Cultural History of the Senses* (2014a), is the leading exponent of the sensualization of historical inquiry (Classen 2001) and has also written a foundational essay on the anthropology of the senses (Classen 1997). In *Worlds of Sense* ([1993a] 2023) she brings out how different cultures and historical periods privilege different senses and the implications these differing 'sensory models' or arrangements have for the deployment of the senses in practice. For example, the cosmology of the Tzotzil of the Chiapas Highlands of Mexico is a thermal cosmology. The Tzotzil conceive of the directions in terms of contrasting temperatures (East is 'Rising Heat', West is 'Waning Heat') as well as social statuses (women are cool, men are hot and senior men are the hottest of all). Plants are classified by temperature (potatoes, which grow in the ground, are cold; maize, which grows toward the sun, is hot) and so too are colours distinguished and categorized by temperature. This may be considered a third case of 'seeing feelingly' (or at least thermally).

The *Cultural History of the Senses* set is noteworthy for the way it departs from the unimodal histories of the senses that predominated during the first phase of the sensory turn, texts such as Corbin's *The Foul and the Fragrant* (Corbin 1986) and *Village Bells* (Corbin 1998), as well as the numerous cultural histories of vision (Jay 1993; Levin 1993; Halpern 2015), hearing (Burnett et al.

1991) and so on. The six volumes of the *Cultural History of the Senses* focus, respectively, on Antiquity (Toner 2014), the Middle Ages (Newhauser 2014), the Renaissance (Roodenburg 2014), the Enlightenment (Vila 2014), the nineteenth century or 'Age of Empire' (Classen 2014b) and the twentieth century or 'Modern Age' (Howes 2014). Each volume is divided into nine chapters or 'domains': the social life of the senses, urban sensations, the marketplace, religion, philosophy and science, medicine, literature, art and media. This domain-based approach foregrounds the shifting relationships among the senses, rather than treating them severally, or one at a time.

Thanks to this ninefold arrangement, various patterns of sensory discrimination and interaction become discernible, both within and across each of the domains grouped by period, and across the periods. For example, the cultural importance of vision can be seen to have increased steadily throughout Western history, aided by the invention of such technologies as the printing press, the microscope and the camera. Smell, by contrast, has declined in importance, with its premodern role as a sign of sanctity or sin and as a medium of health or a vector of disease being discarded in modernity. The pleasures of the senses, in turn, have been celebrated (e.g., Romans) or suppressed (e.g., Puritans) by different groups in different periods of history, and ended up being thoroughly commodified (by design and practices of marketing, namely sensory design, sensory marketing) under consumer capitalism. Of particular note is that there has been a marked shift in the visibility and the audibility of subaltern classes, genders and ethnic groups: beginning in the late nineteenth century, such groups passed from being invisible and denied a voice to affirming their presence in public and vociferously contesting stereotypes. These are just some of the many fascinating insights into the shifting balance or modulation of the senses and the impacts of new techniques and technologies of perception that a close reading of the volumes in the *Cultural History of the Senses* set can yield.

Were earlier eras more alive to sensory experience than today? According to the sociologist Richard Sennett, they were. In *Flesh and Stone: The Body and the City in Western Civilization* (Sennett 1994), he contrasts the sensory vitality of Athens during its golden age (the political culture centring on the agora, the physical culture, the architecture) with the 'tactile sterility' of the modern urban environment, with its towering skyscrapers clad in glass in the urban centre and its rows upon rows of identical single-family dwelling units in suburbia. According to Sennett, urban sprawl disperses the population – thus increasing interpersonal distance – while the various modern 'technologies of motion', such as cars, elevators and movie theatres, provide 'freedom from resistance', by insulating bodies from their surroundings and whisking them from point to point. This 'freedom from resistance' increases passivity, diminishes empathy and undermines meaningful engagement in public life (the domain of alterity) by dulling touch.

The individuation or 'bureaucratization' (Jones 2005) of the senses was otherwise aided by the invention of the concert hall, which took the place of the pub or parlour, as discussed by James Johnson in *Listening in Paris* (Johnson 1996; see further Shaw-Miller 2013), and of the museum as the most suitable place in which to experience (view) art, natural specimens and exotic (ethnographic) artifacts. In the seventeenth and eighteenth centuries, though, the museum was not the hands-off space we know today, geared to the production of 'single sense epiphanies' (Kirshenblatt-Gimblett 1998). Rather, it was a kind of sensory gymnasium, with visitors hefting exhibits to assess their weight, stroking them to feel their textures and even tasting them to determine their chemical composition (Classen 2007).

In *Museum Bodies* (Leahy 2012), Helen Rees Leahy recounts how the bodies and the senses of all classes of society, especially the masses, came to be subdued and regulated and the 'correct comportment' for the appreciation of art came to be instilled, such as walking at a respectful pace (no running) and pausing before each painting.[19] No longer permitted were picnicking in the galleries and children playing in the corners (see further Classen 2017, 2020). The restrictions on the sense of touch (due to the perceived danger it posed to the integrity of the museum pieces) were especially onerous. Only connoisseurs and curators were allowed to handle the exhibits because they could do so 'knowingly' (Candlin 2010). This elitism came to be challenged toward the end of the twentieth century on account of its exclusivity and the way it marginalized sectors of the populace, such as the vision and/or mobility impaired. The work of such organizations as Art Education for the Blind (1998–9) is noteworthy in this connection. These organizations took up the cause of rendering works from Western art history accessible to the visually impaired by, among other things, creating tactile representations of paintings by means of raised dots, lines, cross-hatching and so on, enabling the blind person to feel the painting. Here, then, is a fourth case of 'seeing feelingly'.

The fifth example of cross- or intermodal perception to be considered here is synaesthesia, which was first documented in 1812 (Dimova 2024). Synaesthesia (literally, union of the senses) involves a sensation in one modality triggering a concurrent sensation in another modality, such as reports of a person tasting shapes or hearing colours (Cytowic 1998; van Campen 2010). Unfortunately, due to the colonization of this field of research by psychologists and

---

[19] It is only by standing directly in front of a painting that the convention (illusion) of linear perspective drawing has its intended effect.

neuroscientists, synaesthesia has been reduced to a congenital condition. There are tests to determine whether an individual is a 'genuine' synesthete or simply speaking 'metaphorically' (synaesthesia as 'figure of speech'), or even just 'pretending' (Baron-Cohen et al. 1987). At the same time, emboldened by advances in neurobiology enabled by brain-imaging technologies, such as the finding that colour-grapheme synaesthesia can (hypothetically) be explained as a product of 'the cross-activation of brain maps', researchers such as V. S. Ramachandran and colleagues have proposed that synaesthesia (that is, congenital or 'strong' synaesthesia) be regarded as vital to creativity and 'may provide a crucial insight into some of the most elusive questions about the mind, such as the neural substrate (and evolution) of metaphor, language and thought itself' (Ramachandran et al. 2004: 881).

In keeping with the 'neuromaniacal' (Tallis 2011; Howes 2023) research program of Ramachandran and company, the term synaesthesia has come to be bandied about quite indiscriminately, and extended to encompass many cases which should properly be considered instances of 'crossmodal correspondences' (Spence 2018), such as the general tendency to associate higher-pitch sounds with brighter colours. This tendency, which is not automatic, not idiosyncratic, not necessarily conscious and not 'perceptually real' (all criteria used to determine 'genuineness'),[20] can be enucleated far more economically as a product of perceptual *experience* – that is, as acquired or learned instead of hard-wired or innate. Consider the screech of chalk on a blackboard that sends shivers down your spine, or the relative weight of the vocables 'pong' and 'ping' (Which is heavier, ping or pong?). These are all examples of everyday crossmodal conjunctures. There is no need to recur to 'extraperceptual' (O'Callaghan 2019: 17, 78, 87–8), cognitive or neurological considerations to make sense of them. Ophelia Deroy and Charles Spence (2013a, 2013b) have convincingly argued for researchers to stop assimilating crossmodal correspondences to canonical synaesthesia, since the differences are no less salient (and potentially revealing) than the similarities, and deserve study in their own right. It is categorically wrong-headed to classify crossmodal correspondences as synaesthesias of the 'weak' variety.

The neuroreductionism of the prevailing definition of synaesthesia (in both its 'strong' and its 'weak' varieties) has also been challenged by cultural historians and cultural anthropologists, who point to examples of crossmodal associations that fall outside the ken of neurobiology, such as smelling colour. An example of what it might mean to 'see smellingly' (or scented sight) is

---

[20] The term 'perceptually real' refers to the 'subjective indistinguishability' of the joint sensation: that is, for the synesthete with coloured hearing, the perception of a C sharp *is* bright blue, not *like* bright blue – the equivalence is *total* (see Howes 2023: 157–9).

presented by Diana Young in 'The smell of greenness' (Young 2005). Young carried out ethnographic field research among the Anangu Pitjantjatjara people who inhabit the Anilalya Homelands near Ernabella in the Western Desert of Australia.

> The earth in the Western Desert is red but after heavy or prolonged rain, and the immediate germination of opportunistic seeds, the ground begins to turn a brilliant green. As the first raindrops hit the ground, a strong smell is released. ... Like all odour it is difficult to describe; eucalyptus with a top note of dust and shit – perhaps dog, camel or human. This is my description; Anangu merely describe it as a good smell – *panti wiru*, and one that makes it easier to breath [*sic*]. The smell of eucalyptus is an iconic odour for Anangu. The fragrance emitted by [such eucalypts as] blood wood and red river gum trees [as well as wild tobacco] intensifies during rain as the volatile oils from their leaves are washed from the ground. Anangu link the particular smell of the eucalypt oil washed from the earth as rain falls, and odours they regard as similar, with the transformation of country to green. (Young 2005: 64)

For Anangu, then, bright greens are 'synonymous with water and times of plenty', and there is 'a crucial connection of greenness and life' in that

> Greenness is indicative of the well-being of land and all creatures who live on it including humans. Intensely bright green plants especially are expected to possess a strong smell while the odour itself is expected to promote greenness. Greenness is also ingested. A person can herself become green by consuming very green plants with a strong smell and by rubbing the odour of greenness on her skin. (Young 2005: 64–5)

Greenness and its attendant smells form part of an intersensorial complex that has ancestral and cosmological resonances. According to Anangu cosmogony, the features of the landscape, including waterholes, were created by ancestral beings during a primordial period known as *tjurku* (glossed as Dreamtime in English), when they moved across the land, laying down songlines, and at last went into the ground or up into the sky. There is a far stronger connection between people and country among the autochthonous Anangu than in the dominant, settler society of Australia. The land itself is thought of as 'an animated body' and 'surface changes in the appearance of the land are indexical of the enormous power that the ancestors exert from beneath and through the ground' (Young 2005: 66; see further Biddle 2007).

Young observes: 'Through the songs, dances, stories and material culture of living human beings bequeathed from the Ancestors and passed on through every generation, ... the Ancestors themselves are brought back into the present during ceremonies' (Young 2005: 65). Smell plays a key role in such ceremonies: 'women pull up their clothing over their noses to smell themselves'

(Young 2005: 67). People must not wash their body or hair during the days of participation in the Dreaming *inma* (ceremony), only at the finish of it. In this way the body 'accumulates power from the land evoked through the media of song and dance and via body odour combined with the smell of the "bush buta" *irmangku-irmangka'* (Young 2005: 67), or Indigenous pharmacopoeia. This is a good example of 'emplacement', or 'the sensuous interrelationship of body-mind-habitus' (Howes 2005: 7), where the accent is on the situatedness rather than the boundedness of the body as of the self. Smelling greenness is a whole-body experience, a ritualized and social experience, not some 'neuro-logical foible ... unconnected to any social or embodied context', the way neuroscientists would have it (Young 2005: 62).

Young's study underscores yet again the need to cleave to a relational, interactive and social approach to the study of other sensoria. She uses the term 'cultural synaesthesia' to refer to this crossmodal conjuncture of smelling and seeing greenness among the Anganu, the better to challenge neurobiologists to 'get out of their own heads', as it were (Howes 2023: 1–3), and start to see synaesthesia as 'a social and cultural phenomenon', not simply 'a "biological function"' (Young 2005: 64; see further Boddice and Smith 2020: 34–6).[21] Unfortunately, most neuroscientists are so dazzled by the colourful patterns produced by brain-imaging technologies (Dumit 2004; Casini 2021) that they haven't the foggiest notion of what it might mean to see-smell things the way the Anganu do, or smell-hear things the way the Dogon do (see Howes 2022a: 88), and so forth.

Anangu live 'under occupation' (Biddle 2016). Their ancestral territories have been stripped from them; their communities are wracked by drug and alcohol abuse and violence (Douglas 2005); they have been missionized and force-schooled in an alien epistemology in the interests of 'civilization'. The tragic consequences of the 'civilizing process' are evident in the modern practice of petrol sniffing. Sniffing 'nullifies' a person's social smell: 'Sniffers place a can at the neck of their clothing. The gesture is so similar to that of someone inhaling their own body odour that it must be a deliberate replacement of body odour as social connectivity, with petrol' (Young 2005: 67). Sniffers are displaced people, bereft of any social mooring.

---

[21] The theory of 'cultural synaesthesia' was first articulated by Lawrence Sullivan (1986) in an article on the synaesthetic cosmology of the Desana of Colombia, and then taken up and elaborated further in the chapter entitled 'Unravelling synaesthesia' in *Ways of Sensing* (Howes and Classen 2013). The Desana multi- and intersensory vision of the cosmos is inspired by the ritual ingestion of *ayahuasca* (a hallucinogen), under the guidance of a shaman. Ramachandran and colleagues, however, dismiss drug-induced synaesthesia as mere 'sensory confusion' (Ramachandran et al. 2004).

This brings us to *The End of the Cognitive Empire: The Coming of Age of Epistemologies of the South* (Santos 2018), a book by comparative sociologist and legal scholar Boaventura de Sousa Santos.[22] By way of definition, Santos states: 'The epistemologies of the [Global] South concern the production and validation of knowledges anchored in the experiences of resistance of all those social groups that have systematically suffered injustice, oppression, and destruction caused by capitalism, colonialism, and patriarchy' (Santos 2018: 1). By contrast, the epistemologies of the Global North claim objectivity and universality in the name of 'reason' and 'science', which is to say dispassionate, systematic observation and controlled experimentation.

Santos calls the line that divides the two epistemologies 'the abyssal line'. It is profoundly asymmetrical and exclusionary: us/them, scientific/nonscientific (or artisanal) and metropolitan/colonial, including postcolonial (Santos 2018: 21). 'The objective of the epistemologies of the South is to allow the oppressed social groups to represent the world as their own and on their own terms, for only thus will they be able to change it according to their own aspirations' (Santos 2018: 1). That is, only through the decolonization of knowledge and society can the abyssal line be crossed, understood for what it is and overcome. Santos quotes Angela Davis: 'walls turned sideways are bridges' (Santos 2018: 118). Ethnography, or what Santos calls 'intercultural translation' (Santos 2018: 32–4), is crucial to this endeavour.

In chapter 8, 'The deep experience of the senses', Santos enucleates how this bridging can be abetted through the liberation and 'intercrossing' of the senses, a process that begins by 'warming up reason' (*corazonar*) and recognizing that 'all observation is always completed by whatever or whoever is observed' (Santos 2018: 172). Santos stakes out his position as follows: 'The truth is ... that without the senses there are no sensations, without sensations there are no emotions, without emotions there are no perceptions, and without perceptions there would be no world as it presents itself to us and as we present ourselves to it' (Santos 2018: 165).

The deep experience of the senses acknowledges this reciprocity – of seeing and being seen, of hearing and being heard, of feeling and being felt, and of 'feeling-thinking', *corazonar* (Santos 2018: 165, 99–105). Modern science categorically rejects such reciprocity, and it does this in three ways. First, it valorizes the mind over the body (where the senses are localized) – 'Only the

---

[22] *The End of the Cognitive Empire* will disturb your way of thinking if you are of a phenomenological persuasion, after Merleau-Ponty. Santos (2018: 171) writes: 'the problem with Merleau-Ponty's stance is that, quite in tune with Western mores, the theory is formulated as expressing a universal human characteristic that operates in a monotonic way irrespective of contexts, bodily cultures, and power relations among bodies'.

mind knows; only reason is transparent regarding what is known; hence, only reason is trustworthy . . . "it is not the eye that sees, but the mind"' (Santos 2018: 165). Second, it elevates sight and hearing to the top of a hierarchized sensorium 'because they were associated with cognition, while taste, smell, and touch were considered lower senses, particularly developed among the [so-called] lower races' (Santos 2018: 166–7). And third, it adopts the modern 'paradigm of sight' – namely, 'seeing everything without being seen' (Santos 2018: 170). Think of the scientist scrutinizing nature through the lens of a microscope, or of the guards in the observation tower of the Panopticon, Bentham's model prison, who surveil the inmates without being seen in return (Foucault 1977).

The scientist inspecting natural phenomena, like prison guards surveiling inmates, is an example of 'asymmetrical seeing' (Santos 2018: 175), which forms an integral part of the 'political economy of the senses' in metropolitan societies and also informs how colonial societies are viewed from the 'extractivist' perspective of the Global North. It is a binary vision, predicated on the subject–object dichotomy. By contrast, the Anangu of the Western Desert of Australia view the natural world as 'an animated body' (both sensible and sentient). Other examples of such a 'subject–subject philosophy' include the Andean notion of the Pachamama (Mother Earth), 'a non-Cartesian, non-Baconian conception of nature, that is to say, nature not as a natural resource but rather nature as a living being and source of life, to which rights are ascribed as to humans' (as in the Ecuadorian Constitution), and *ubuntu*, 'a southern African idea that calls for an ontology of co-being and coexisting ("I am because we are")' (Santos 2018: 10).

How is it possible to bridge the abyss that separates the epistemologies and the sociabilities of the Global South and the Global North? If I read him correctly, Santos suggests that it involves replacing 'knowing-about' by 'knowing-with' and 'being-with', and abjuring observation-extraction in the interests of promoting participant sensation and intercultural translation. This is the mission of the 'post-abyssal researcher', who must navigate all the asymmetries and incommensurabilities thrown up by the abyssal line, attend to the 'crisscrossed multiplicity of the senses' and strive to 'see on the terms of the other' (Santos 2018: 172).

> There is no uniform system of equivalence for the intercrossing senses. For instance, what the researcher sees in a particular group does not necessarily coincide with what that group sees in the researcher seeing them. Indeed, reciprocity may occur between different senses without those involved noticing it. . . . The researcher may be intent on hearing the group while the group is intent on seeing her. She may be savoring the food she has been offered while whoever offered it is focused on seeing her eat. Reciprocity

involves here two different senses: between hearing and sight or between taste and sight. The intensity of the two intercrossing senses may be equally high. The two senses may flow smoothly or clash and affect each other . . .. (Santos 2018: 166–7)[23]

Santos continues:

> The crisscrossed multiplicity of the senses is one of the most complex topics in social interactions. The same object or practice may be socially constructed to be seen and yet, at a deeper level, it may offer itself to be heard, touched, smelled, or tasted as well. In such cases, a deeper understanding of the object or practice requires the confluence of the various senses. This kind of sensorial depth based on intersensoriality is not compatible with the rationality of Western modernity, since it puts at stake the linearity, unidirectionality, and unidimensionality of extractivist perception. (Santos 2018: 167)

The post-abyssal researcher cultivates the capacity for 'being of two sensoria' by attending to the interrelationships among the senses as among people, and therefore develops the capacity to be of more than one mind about things (Howes 2003: 10–14 and 2022a: 127, 139).[24] The objective is to articulate 'a new common sense' (Santos 2002) which is not beholden to observation, cognition or reason, as defined in the West, but which 'warms up' reason (*corazonar*) in order that we can see and think feelingly (Santos 2018: 97–102).

The question arises: How could science be done differently? That is the subject of Section 5.

Part II Études Sensorielles

5 Doing Science with Margaret Lucas Cavendish: For a Sensuous Epistemology

This section advances three propositions: first, that sensory critique is the beginning of cultural critique; second, that sensory critique is the beginning of epistemological critique; and, third, that a just social and cosmological order is contingent on doing justice to and by other peoples' and creatures' senses, or 'sensory emancipation'. These three propositions, which are all integral to the cross-disciplinary field of sensory studies,[25] will be demonstrated through

---

[23] How beautifully this last point, about the senses 'clashing and affecting each other', echoes McLuhan's notion of the collideroscope of the sensorium!

[24] For a concrete example of Santos' methodology, see the chapter on 'Sensing the social' in *Experience, Caste and the Everyday Social* (Guru and Sarukkai 2019).

[25] These propositions should be read in conjunction with the 'Twelve Propositions for Sensory Studies' put forward in *The Sensory Studies Manifesto* (Howes 2022a: 12–13; see further Howes 2023: 17).

a study of the writings of the seventeenth-century polymath and utopian thinker Margaret Lucas Cavendish (1623–73), Duchess of Newcastle.

Cavendish was a singular figure for many reasons. She was unusual for her time in being a woman who wrote prolifically on many subjects, including natural philosophy, and had her writings *published*.[26] She also commanded attention for her highly public persona: for example, the occasion of her visit to the Royal Society on 30 May 1667 was a public spectacle which attracted quite a crowd (Cavendish was the first woman ever to be invited to a session at this male-only retreat of learning). This celebrity was enhanced by her fashion choices: for example, she wore a knee-length juste-au-corps coat (a style normally worn by men) and an extremely ostentatious train for the aforementioned visit: 'I endeavour to be as singular as I can . . . I had rather appear worse in singularity, than better in the mode' (see Whitaker 2003: 297–305). Furthermore, she questioned the institution of marriage and compulsory heterosexism. Finally, Cavendish had a profound empathy for animals and how animals sense the world: she cultivated a cross-species sensibility.

Cavendish was the youngest of eight children born to the arch Royalist Sir Thomas Lucas and Elizabeth Leighton. She never received any formal education, though she was very studious and did have access to libraries in addition to being lovingly tutored by her brother John Lucas.[27] Following the outbreak of the English Civil War in 1643, she became a maid of honour to Queen Henrietta Maria, who was ensconced at Merton College, Oxford while King Charles I held court at Christ Church.[28] In 1644 she accompanied the Queen into exile in Paris, where she met William Cavendish (1593–1676), the Marquis and later Duke of Newcastle. They married in 1645.

William Cavendish was a renowned horseman (skilled at dressage), a man of letters and a patron of diverse playwrights, such as Ben Jonson, and philosophers, most notably Thomas Hobbes. Indeed, Hobbes, together with the Duke's brother, the distinguished mathematician Sir Charles Cavendish, and

---

[26] On the challenges faced by any premodern woman who elected to take up the pen instead of the needle, see Classen 1998: 86–106 and 2005: 78–82.

[27] Cavendish would later find another male mentor in her brother-in-law, Sir Charles Cavendish (Battigelli 1998: 46–7).

[28] For a description of the Oxford scene in 1643–4, see Whitaker 2003: 47–57. It has been suggested that Cavendish 'came of age' at Merton, during her residency there with Queen Henrietta Maria, whose presence transformed the college into a 'center of female power' (Siegfried and Walters 2022: 2). 'Meanwhile, across Oxford, the wives and daughters of Royalist lords and cavaliers intermingled with soldiers, students, and dons in the once all-male preserve'; this early experience of 'academic intermingling' was quite formative, it seems, since Cavendish would 'reimagine [it] in a variety of literary forms throughout her career' (Siegfried and Walters 2022: 2). Incidentally, Merton College admitted its first female cohort of undergraduate students in 1980 and appointed its first female warden, Professor Dame Jessica Rawson, in 1994. This restoration was a long time coming.

the writer Sir Kenelm Digby, formed the nucleus of the Cavendish Circle in Paris. The circle also attracted René Descartes and Pierre Gassendi, among other continental philosophers. While Margaret Cavendish was not included in the discussions of these virtuosi when they came to dine, she read their works and would go on to tangle with their ideas in her own writing. One way in which she did this was through penning a series of letters – *Philosophical Letters* (Cavendish 1664b) – addressed to an imaginary 'Madam'. She thus transformed the masculine philosophical dialogue of the time into a feminine or cross-sex dialogue in which she could have an important say (see further Cunning 2022).

During the Interregnum, the couple moved to Amsterdam and then Antwerp, where they were able to maintain an aristocratic lifestyle thanks to the Duke's skill at arranging loans (with no collateral, only his reputation, to speak of). After the Stuart Restoration in 1660, the couple returned to England. William Cavendish's estate (which had been sequestered by the Commonwealth forces) was restored, but neither Fortune nor the King saw fit to bestow on him the office he (and Margaret) thought he deserved on account of his unswerving loyalty and military service during the Civil War.[29] So the couple took up residence together with William Cavendish's four children by a previous marriage (all older than Margaret herself) at his country estate, Welbeck. The couple remained childless, which enabled Cavendish to pass her time in her study reading voraciously and writing profusely. Her books, she felt, would not only disseminate her ideas in her own time but also provide her with a kind of literary immortality to which women rarely had access (see Figure 1).[30]

Though happily married herself (William Cavendish was a devoted husband, who underwrote the publication of her literary and philosophical works, in addition to penning prefaces which extolled her intellect and virtue), Margaret was highly critical of the institution of marriage, just as she was critical of women's exclusion from the masculine world of learning or 'science' and politics. This came to a head in her play *The Convent of Pleasure* (1668; see Cavendish [1668] 1999). The play opens with a discussion among a group of gentlemen, who have designs on the recently widowed Lady Happy. They are desirous of her beauty, her reproductive

---

[29] This was a sore point for Cavendish, but (by teaming up with Honesty and Prudence) she bested Fortune (and her cronies Folly and Rashness) in the debate scene (presided over by Truth) near the end of *Blazing World* (Cavendish [1666b] 2016: 133–9), at least on paper.

[30] The recognition Cavendish craved and pursued so relentlessly finally came, ca. 300 years later, with the 1990s 'Cavendish Renaissance'. Many feminist and other scholars started to celebrate the Duchess' work for the way she experimented with mixing genres and crossing genders (Rees 2003; Pohl 2003; Bonin 2009; Walters 2009), gave the practice of natural philosophy a different voice and advocated for female emancipation – to a degree. It must be said that Cavendish consistently wavered between challenging and supporting conventional notions of femininity, making it difficult to determine her 'feminist credentials' from a contemporary perspective (Boyle 2004; Sarasohn 2009; Keller 2009).

Figure 1 Effigy of Margaret Lucas Cavendish with book and inkhorn, Westminster Abbey.

Source: Copyright © Dean and Chapter of Westminster, London.

power and principally her property as means to their own aggrandizement. Enter Lady Happy, who declares that women of her station 'were mad to live with Men, who make the Female Sex their slaves' (Cavendish [1668] 1999: 220). She resolves to found a convent and proceeds to take in 'so many Noble Persons of my Own Sex' as her estate can support: 'with them I mean to live incloister'd with all the delights and pleasures that are allowable and lawful; My Cloister shall not be a Cloister of restraint but a place for freedom, not to vex the Senses but to please them' (Cavendish [1668] 1999: 220).

The convent is a women's college, or 'school for the senses' (Siegfried 2006: 72), dedicated to the observation of nature in all her variety, with Lady Happy as its warden. The convent has 'much compass of ground' within its walls ('place enough for Gardens, Orchards, Walks, Groves, Bowers, Arbours, Ponds, Fountains, Springs, and the like'), while its bed chambers are ordered 'according to the Four Seasons of the year': 'As in the Spring, our Chambers are hung with Silk-Damask, and all other things suitable to it; and a great Looking-Glass in each Chamber, that we may view ourselves and take pleasure in our own Beauties, whilst they are fresh and young [like the spring season] also' (Cavendish [1668] 1999: 223). So too with the women's garments, their plate, their victuals, their drink (hot in winter, cool in summer), their bed linen and their decorations (perfumes, pictures and wall-hangings – taffeta in summer, tapestry in winter). All these 'Varieties' meant that it would 'require a long time' to know them and 'their several Changes' (Cavendish [1668] 1999: 226).

A while later, another group of 'monsieurs', hanging out outside the convent, are miffed at having their gaze blocked: 'But is there no place where we may peak into the Convent?' one asks; 'No, there are no grates, but Brick and

Stone-walls', another observes (Cavendish [1668] 1999: 227). They then plot to have the convent disbanded (by torching it if necessary), but are forestalled by the arrival of 'a great Foreign Princess . . . of a Masculine Presence' (Cavendish [1668] 1999: 225–6), and dare not.

Within the convent, it is customary for some women to dress and behave like masculine 'servants' to others, and even to play at courting.[31] The Princess requests and is permitted to do likewise (dress like a man and 'serve' Lady Happy). For each other's amusement and instruction, the women put on plays, some of which dramatize the subjection and vexation of 'mean' (read: lower-class) women by their husbands, while others depict noble women being crossed (Cavendish [1668] 1999: 220–34). The Princess professes to be 'unconvinced', but then gets caught up in the action when invited to play Neptune to Lady Happy's sea goddess.

Lady Happy finds that she has fallen in love with the Princess, which plunges her into a melancholic state: 'My name is *Happy*, and so was my Condition, before I saw this Princess; but now I am like to be the most unhappy Maid alive: But why may I not love a Woman with the same affection I could a Man?' (Cavendish [1668] 1999: 234). Such a match would be considered against nature, but then events reveal that the 'Princess' is actually a prince, which allows the pair to marry (naturally enough). This leads to the dissolution of the convent (it becoming the Prince's property upon marriage). By means of this finale or denouement, Cavendish is able to stay on the 'right' side of public morality while craftily introducing an alternative vision of society.

The Convent of Pleasure can be read as addressing the opposing topoi of 'the banquet of intellect' and 'the banquet of sense'. This opposition was framed by William Shakespeare and Ben Jonson in their plays, as well as George Chapman in his Christian adaptation of Ovid's ode to his mistress (from the *Metamorphosis*) entitled *Ovid's Banquet of Sense* (Chapman [1595] 2014). It turns on the opposition between Plato's *Symposium* and Circe's cup – or, in Christian terms, partaking of the Lord's table (the Eucharist) versus Paul's 'table of demons' (1 Corinthians 10: 21), and heavenly love versus carnal lust, if one follows Kermode (1971; but see also Vinge 1975). The idea is that a soul (if it be virtuous) will ascend and transcend the senses to achieve knowledge and blissful union with God, or else revel in them and be damned.[32]

---

[31] There really is 'no occasion for Men' (Cavendish [1668] 1999: 223), then, and it bears noting that Lady Happy 'has also Women-Physicians, Surgeons and Apothecaries' (Cavendish [1668] 1999: 223) – that is, the convent is exclusively staffed by female professionals.

[32] The sequence of courses (read: senses) at these banquets admits of some variation, and the shuffling of sensations that goes on in these variations is laced with significance (see Vinge 1975). Incidentally, Cavendish experimented with this topos again in one of her letters. The setting is rather grisly (the table is made of 'Famous Old Poets Sculs' draped with a cloth spun

However, a close reading of the play reveals some significant variations on this topos. First, all the maids and widows who make up Lady Happy's company vow to remain chaste, and there is an extended discussion of love and friendship that borders on the Platonic: it centres on the issue of what's in a kiss between female friends (Cavendish [1668] 1999: 234). Second, it is not as though the pleasures of the senses are pursued wantonly; they are sought only to a degree that is 'allowable and lawful' (Cavendish [1668] 1999: 220). Third, the convent is a space dedicated to contemplating and participating in the beauty and the endless creativity of nature. It is just that the science practised within its walls – a 'science of sensible qualities' (Lévi-Strauss and Eribon 2018; Lévi-Strauss 2020; Howes 2023: ch. 4) – does not have the knowledge and the love of God, or some rarefied conception of the intellect, as its endpoint. This foreclosure stems from the fact that, in Cavendish's materialist universe (on which more presently), God, being 'Immaterial', is not knowable. Specifically, knowledge of God is a matter of faith, and therefore is beyond 'Sense and Reason' (Siegfried and Sarasohn 2014).

Brandie Siegfried suggests that the publication of *The Convent of Pleasure* represented an 'enthusiastic thrust' against the champions of the New Science, such as Thomas Sprat, co-founder and chronicler of the Royal Society (established in 1660). These New Scientists 'portray the "masculine" arts of knowledge as a superior and positive alternative to the [supposedly] morally and intellectually inferior "feminine" arts of pleasure' (Siegfried 2006: 65). For Cavendish, by contrast, who 'folds the arts of delight back into the practice of moral and philosophical reason ... aesthetically tutored senses not only *warm the intellect* to true insight, but make possible the cognitive leap from the limitations of present epistemes to new realms of knowledge' (Siegfried 2006: 65, emphasis added; compare Santos 2018 on *corazonar*).

The New Science had itself introduced an epistemic rupture that also centred on the senses. In place of deferring to the writings of the Ancients, such as Aristotle, and the deductive syllogisms of the Scholastics, the New Scientists (Robert Boyle, Francis Bacon, Robert Hooke, etc.) proceeded experimentally and inductively. Their inductive empiricism involved 'turning the five senses into replicable universal tools' (Kettler 2021: 180) by instrumentalizing them – as in the way 'Optick-Glasses' (microscopes, telescopes) objectify vision; elaborating a 'plain style' language and using diagrams to record their observations (Nate 2009); and, on this basis, prying into and laying bare the 'secrets' of

---

from 'Old Poets Brains', while 'Orators Tongues' serve as knives, etc.), but the fare is quite refined: the first course is 'a Great Dish of Poems' with a 'Curious Sawce made of Metaphors, Similitudes, and Fancies', there is a 'Hash of Anagrams' and even a 'Dish of Epithalamiums', and so on (Cavendish [1664a] 1997: 212–14).

nature. Their plain language could not have been more different from Cavendish's florid prose, just as their gaze could not have been more stereotypically masculine. This gaze was exemplified by Robert Hooke's (1665) magnum opus *Micrographia*, with its detailed depictions of nature under a magnifying lens. Hooke framed the blow-ups of minuscule creatures (fleas, flies) in the *Micrographia* as correcting for the limitations and distortions of the unaided eyes, which he deemed to be wanting 'a full sensation of the Object', and endeavoured to instead disclose 'the true nature of the things themselves' (quoted in Clucas 2022: 53).

Hooke's celebration of the revelatory powers of the microscope agreed with Francis Bacon's program in the *Novum Organon*, the charter of the new experimental science. The Baconian program staked its truth claims on procedural objectivity and the value-neutrality of its findings, while holding out the promise of intellectual and material progress or 'the relief of man's estate' as its outcome (see generally Merchant 1980; Jordanova 1989). Tellingly, Bacon averred that 'nature exhibits herself more clearly under the *trials* and *vexations* of [experimentation] than when left to herself' (cited in Classen 2005: 77).

But Cavendish, in her defence of (an increasingly outmoded) natural philosophy, grounded in 'Sense and Reason' rather than scientific instruments, has a riposte for all these masculine machinations.[33] In her view, nature is lively (or 'self-moving'), all-knowing and eminently industrious. Indeed, as she argues in *Observations upon Experimental Philosophy*:

> Nature, being a wise and provident lady, governs her parts very wisely, methodically and orderly; Also she is very industrious, and hates to be idle, which makes her employ her time as a good housewife doth, in brewing, baking, churning, spinning, sewing, etc., as also in preserving . . . for she has numerous employments; and being infinitely self-moving, never wants work but her artificial works are her works of delight, pleasure and pastime. (Cavendish [1666a] 2001: 105)

Cavendish goes on to draw out the implications of the isomorphism between nature's works or workings and women's work for the practice of experimental science:

> my opinion is, that our female sex would be the fittest for it; for they most commonly take pleasure in making of sweetmeats, possets, several sorts of pies, puddings, and the like; not so much for their own eating, as to employ their idle time; and it may be, they would prove good experimental

---

[33] The point of the discussion that follows is that the senses are gendered socially (Classen 1998) just as the mind is sexed (Schiebinger 1989; Jordanova 1989), despite all Bacon and company's paeans to the neutrality of scientific instruments, the objectification of knowing and the 'eventual comprehensiveness of theory' (Keller 2009: 175).

philosophers, and inform the world how to make artificial snow, by their creams, or possets beaten into froth: and ice, by their clear, candied, or crusted quiddities, or conserves of fruits; ... and hail, by their small comfits made of water and sugar, with whites of eggs: And many other the like figures, which resemble beasts, birds, vegetables, minerals, etc. (Cavendish [1666a] 2001: 105–6; see further Sarasohn 2009: 140; Siegfried 2003: 62–7)

As Classen (1998: 104) observes, Cavendish's 'homey portrayals of science served to diminish the masculine majesty of the field and bring it within the domestic realm of women'. Her proposal for the desegregation of science is extremely bold and potentially fruitful, or could have been had she not gone on to depict women's role as limited to serving as lab assistants (which freed up the male scientists to theorize causes) in conformity to the idea that 'woman was given to man not onely to delight, but to help and assist him' (Cavendish [1666a] 2001: 106).

Margaret Cavendish's first published work was entitled *Poems, and Fancies* (Cavendish 1653). Her attitude toward the natural world, as expressed in this work, contrasted with that of the members of the Royal Society, particularly as regards the treatment of animals. While the scientists ruthlessly tortured animals in their quest for knowledge – and even for entertainment – Cavendish was disposed to empathize with animals as sensitive beings who merit consideration and respect. Thus, in *A Dialogue Betwixt Man and Nature*, she has Nature declare that '*beasts* have *life* and *sense*, and *passion* strong / Yet *cruel man* doth kill and doth them wrong' (Cavendish 1653: 59). Her poem *The Hunting of the Hare* elaborates on this point:

> As if that *God* made *Creatures* for *Mans meat*,
> To give them *Life*, and *Sense*, for *Man* to eat;
> Or else for *Sport*, or *Recreations* sake,
> Destroy those *Lifes* that *God* saw good to make:
> Making their *Stomacks, Graves*, which full they fill
> With *Murther'd Bodies*, that in sport they kill.
> (Cavendish 1653: 112)

This poem nicely exemplifies Cavendish's propensity for thinking and feeling across boundaries, here the putative boundary between species (see further Battigelli 1998: 122–4).

In another poem, Cavendish entertains the idea (popular at the time) that the world is composed of four differently shaped kinds of atoms (square for earth, round for water, long for air, sharp for fire), each one 'eternal and infinite', and each acting of its own volition: 'Such *Formes* as best agree, make every kinde ... / So *Atomes*, as they dance, finde places fit ... / And thus, by chance, may a New *World* create' (Cavendish 1653: 5). This atomic, or 'corpuscular', cosmology bordered on the heretical since, according to Christian notions, only God is eternal and infinite, He is the prime architect and mover of the universe, and all worldly things and beings are subject to His providential plan. This heterodoxy is further emphasized in another poem when Margaret suggests 'that there are an infinity of worlds, probably populated, not only outside our world but inside it as well, for instance within a lady's earring: "And if thus small, then ladies well might weare / A world of worlds, as pendants in each eare"' (Sarasohn 2009: 135; see further Battigelli 1998: ch. 3).

As her confidence in her own writing (and the rightness of her own specula-tions) grew, Cavendish went from composing poetry to writing philosophy, frequently using satire to highlight the presumptuousness of her male peers, who set themselves up as 'petty gods' (Cavendish [1666a] 2001: 112; Keller 2009; Hutton 2003) – that is, 'outside of nature' (Kettler 2021: 180). She mocked the usefulness of their experiments, which were 'routinely under attack for not producing incontestable results' while generating more discord than they did truth (Keller 2009: 174). Above all, she criticized her male counterparts for their narrow outlook: 'although each particular creature or part of Nature may have some conception of the Infinite parts of Nature, yet it can not know the truth of those Infinite parts, being but a finite part itself, which finiteness causes errors in perception' (Cavendish [1666a] 2001: 48; see Keller 2009: 181; James 2009).

This critique came to a head in a story Cavendish published in 1666 entitled *The Description of a New World Called the Blazing World* (as a companion to the *Observations*), where she directly confronts the masculine scientific estab-lishment, with its cult of 'Optick Glasses'. The story begins with a maiden being kidnapped and transported aboard a boat bound for the North Pole. After various mishaps (which leave her male captors dead), she steps into a parallel universe illuminated by blazing stars and peopled by anthropomorphic animals (Bird-men, Spider-men, Bear-men and so on). In short order, she marries the Emperor and is proclaimed the Empress of this New World. She then goes about dividing the populace into schools and learned societies: the Bird-men become astronomers, the Spider-men mathematicians, the Ape-men chemists, Worm-men geologists, the Bear-men experimental philosophers – and proceeds to interrogate them for their wisdom.

Significantly, the Empress upbraids the Bear-men for their reliance on optic glasses:

> In *Blazing World* the bear-men scientists try to understand nature by examin-ing it through telescopes and microscopes. It soon becomes evident, however,

that such magnifying lenses have a series of deficiencies which lead them to present a grossly distorted image of the world. For example, lenses can produce a magnified image of a louse, but not of a whale, they can operate in light but not in darkness, they can enhance one sense but are no use to any of the others. "Your glasses are false informers, and instead of discovering the truth, delude your senses," the Empress proclaims. "Wherefore I command you to break them." (Classen 1998: 104)

Later, the Empress relents in the face of all the Bear-men's protests and 'allows the experimenters to keep their lenses with the condition that they not cause any public disturbance' – then, as 'a final jab at the delusions of scientists who imagine that all mysteries can be comprehended through extending the power of sight, Cavendish leaves her experimental philosophers trying to invent a magnifying glass by means of which "they could spy out a vacuum"' (Classen 1998: 104).

There is a world of difference between the sensuous epistemology and the vital materialist cosmology of Cavendish's mature writings (Sarasohn 2003) and the sensationist philosophy and the mechanical cosmology of the Royal Society. This difference centres on her understanding of nature as constituting a self-moving, all-knowing and endlessly creative living whole. In contrast to the atomism of her earlier writings[34] and the mechanical materialism of the Royal Society and of the philosopher Thomas Hobbes, Cavendish's materialism is organic, or 'vital'. According to her tripartite scheme, nature is composed of rational animate matter, sensitive animate matter and inanimate matter, but all three are 'co-mixt', so nothing is inert, nothing is not sentient and nothing is not rational to some degree – from minerals and medicines to organisms (both animal and human) and from each one of an organism's organs to nature as a whole (Cavendish [1666a] 2001:72, 99, 149–54 and 1664b: 107, 115; Sarasohn 2003). This is a vibrant universe indeed, since *everything* participates in a dynamic, responsive whole.

Cavendish's epistemology is of a piece with this ontology. According to her voluntarist theory of perception, sensations are not attributable to the 'pressure' that one body exerts on another, as Hobbes presumed (James 2009). Rather, each component part of nature 'patterns out' the motions of those other parts of nature it comes into contact with, and *elects* to move itself accordingly, harmoniously – or not (Cunning 2022). The idea here is of perception as a kind of empathic autokinesis. The deterministic notion of natural laws is foreign to this conception, which plays up the ineluctability of choice, instead. Living in the

---

[34] Cavendish appears to have gone off atomism primarily on account of its political implications. As a Royalist, she was a lifelong defender of the sovereignty of the monarchy, not the individual (James 2009; Sarasohn 2009: 138–43; Boyle 2018).

material world entails being sensitive – which is to say responsive to, as Cavendish puts it, the 'Sense and Reason, Life and Knowledge' of all creation (see Cavendish 1664b: 187 and [1666a] 2001: 82, 100).

To circle back to our discussion in Section 1, it is instructive to compare Cavendish's theory of perception and cognition with '4E Cognition Theory', which comes out of contemporary cognitive neuroscience. The 4E theory has its roots in the concept of the embodied mind advanced by Francisco Varela, Eleanor Rosch and Evan Thompson (Varela et al. [1991] 2017), and stands for Embodied, Embedded, Extended and Enacted (see generally Aagard 2021; Chemero 2009; Shapiro and Spaulding 2021). This theory departs from Descartes' separation of mind and body by fusing the two, and it departs from Locke's depiction of the senses as passive receptors by representing perception as a form of action, or 'enaction' (hence, performative). As appears from the foregoing discussion of the sensuous epistemology of the Duchess of Newcastle, these notions were already present, ca. 300 years earlier, in Cavendish's materialist theory of the cosmos (including the mind or soul) and her dynamic theory of perception as 'patterning out' (i.e., the sensitive and rational parts of one self-moving part of nature replicating the exterior motions of another to achieve cognition).

However, Cavendish's theory was also rather more capacious than 4E Cognition Theory, both in its pluralism and in its holism. It is more holistic because Cavensish would never have subscribed to the so-called extended mind hypothesis (Clarke 2008), which continues to take human cognition as its touchstone even as it purports to be 'extracranial' (Aagard 2021).[35] For her, all-knowing nature is already in mind. It is not a question of the 'distribution of cognition' as in the way a notebook functions as an 'extension' of cerebral processes (i.e., a projection of the mind in nature) according to the extended mind hypothesis, for the latter remains anthropocentric, whereas Margaret's theory is cosmomorphic.

As regards the pluralism of Cavendish's theory of perception and cognition, it is noteworthy that she

> disagreed with the opinion [attributed to Descartes] that 'all knowledg is in the Mind and none in the senses.' Cavendish argued that each part of the body and each sense has its own knowledge: 'the Eye is as knowing as the Ear, and the Ear as knowing as the Nose, and the Nose as knowing as the Tongue.'

---

[35] The concept of embeddedness might seem similar to that of emplacement (discussed below), but it falls short since it hinges on projection or planting (i.e., insertion), typically by means of technology, rather than the introjection of nature's wisdom, and reciprocation.

She similarly stated in favour of a bodily intelligence that, 'The Heads Braines cannot ingross all knowledge to themselves'. (Classen 1998: 101)

This radical decentring of intelligence is further emphasized in the notion of a fifth E, as it were – namely 'emplacement' – 'the sensuous interrelationship of body-mind-habitus' (Howes 2005: 7). Recall how the senses (and the resulting knowledges) of the animal scientists in *Blazing World* are each fitted to and conditioned by their respective sensory environments (Kettler 2021: 180–5) or *Umwelten* (von Uexküll 2018): 'each followed such a profession as was most proper for the nature of their species' (Cavendish [1666b] 2016: 71). This is, of course, another jab at the visualism of the Royal Society, but it is also more than that: it underscores the cultural-environmental contingency of perception and cognition. From the monistic, know-it-all position of the male scientists of her day, Cavendish's insistence on the diversity of ways of sensing and the concomitant limits of knowing, and her imaginative style, did not sit well, and her tracts were accordingly spurned. It is doubtful whether her philosophy of mind would fare any better in the face of the 'neuromaniacal' perspective of contemporary cognitive scientists (Tallis 2011).

To conclude, Margaret Lucas Cavendish challenged the gender constraints of seventeenth-century England to develop and disseminate her own views on many of the key social and scientific concepts of the day. She critiqued contemporary notions of women and animals as 'mindless', and envisioned alternate worlds in which other social orders could flourish. She signalled with humour and insight the underlying prejudices in the premises and practices of the male scientists of the day and the narrowness of the channels in which their imaginations ran. This critique is brilliantly summed up in the opposition between the Looking-Glasses in the chambers of the Convent of Pleasure and the Optick-Glasses in the showrooms of the Royal Society. The mirror, typically a symbol of female vanity, is construed very differently by Cavendish; for her, *the* instrument of vanity is the microscope, while the mirror stands for self-knowledge.

There is a direct link between the modes of mastering the world promoted by the Royal Society and the catastrophic conditions (both ecological and social) in which we find our planet and ourselves in the present. Approaching the world according to the more sensitive, egalitarian and interdependent models proposed by Cavendish would enable us to understand the *interconnectedness* and *interactivity* of all things (Haraway 1988, 2016; see further Walters 2009: 260); recognize the *vibrancy* of the material world (Bennett 2010); and 'meet the universe halfway' (Barad 2007). Doing science

Cavendish's way also has the potential to wean us from being overly beholden to vision and help us start to *appreciate the differences* among the senses as alternate ways of knowing and being (Fox Keller and Grontkowski 1983; Howes 2022a, 2023).[36]

As Eve Keller (2009: 191) observes, Margaret Cavendish was 'uniquely aware of the gendered construction of the new science *as it was being created*: its binary categories – of observer and observed, subject and object, truth and fiction, philosophy and fantasy – were to Cavendish's mind necessary finally not for discovering that "one truth of nature," but rather for producing men as "petty gods"'. Thus, Cavendish's feminine sensuous epistemology could have laid the groundwork for an alternate science of nature, keyed to the notion of a 'sensitive ecology' (Classen 2023). It promoted reflexivity regarding the limits of knowing in place of objectivity, and complexity in place of unity – the 'one truth of nature'. The cosmology she sketched in *Blazing World* ran contrary to Bacon's *Novum Organum*. It could have flourished as a counterpart to the latter, but the masculine scientific establishment of the day was too closed-minded and self-centred to allow that to happen.

As Classen observes regarding Cavendish's notorious effrontery and pluralism of mind:[37]

> It was not only the fact of Margaret Cavendish's writing which challenged contemporary norms, but her style of writing. Cavendish tended to present all opinions and conventions, including her own, as hypotheses which could be accepted, rejected or transformed by the reader. . . . Although Cavendish was by no means free of social prejudices herself, her ultimate vision was of a world in which women and men are not obliged to conform to a repressive external standard of behavior but can create their own identities. (Classen 1998: 106)

This opening of the imagination and the senses to alterity is summed up in the closing lines of *Blazing World*, where Cavendish declares her 'ambition' to be 'Authoress of a whole World' (and clearly identifies with the Empress as alter ego, or soul-mate), then goes on to state: 'if any should like the World I have made, and be willing to be my Subjects, they may imagine themselves such . . . but if they cannot endure to be subjects, they may create Worlds of their own, and Govern themselves as they please' (Cavendish [1666b] 2016: 163).

---

[36] Karen Barad, Jane Bennett, Donna Haraway, Evelyn Fox Keller and Christine Grontkowski are all female thinkers at the forefront of contemporary science and technology studies.

[37] For an illuminating account of Cavendish's mental pluralism, see Stevenson 2009.

6 Painting with James McNeill Whistler: A Sensory Biography of the Artist's Works and Life

This section offers a sensory biography of the works and life of the expatriate American painter James McNeill Whistler (1834–1903). It opens with a definition of the terms that frame the following account, starting with 'sensory biography'. This concept was introduced by the anthropologist Robert Desjarlais (2003) in his ethnographic study of the life stories of two elders of the Yolmo wa ethnic group of the Nepal Himalayas. A sensory biography may be likened to a psychobiography, such as Freud's famous analysis of Leonardo da Vinci (Freud 1953–74, vol. 6). However, its focus is on the sense life of the individual in contrast to Freud's unswerving (reductionist) focus on the sex life.[38]

People have biographies and so do things, according to the anthropologist Igor Kopytoff in a seminal chapter of *The Social Life of Things* (Appadurai 1986). Kopytoff (1986) notes how things change hands and become storied as aspects of their 'cultural biography'. I would add that the *agencement* (commonly translated as 'assemblage' but also hinting at the idea of agency) of things also has a sensory dimension; for example the way 'exotic' artifacts come to be exhibited behind glass in the display cases of the museum, which seriously curtails the sensory life they lived in their cultures of provenance. In what follows the accent will accordingly be on the 'sensori-social life of things' (Howes 2006, 2022b) – most notably, Whistler's paintings and lithographs and his collection of Asian artifacts and prints.[39]

The other term of cardinal importance to the following analysis is 'emplacement'. This concept introduced a refinement to the notion of 'embodiment' (Csordas 1990). The latter concept was mobilized in the critique of the dualism of mind and body in the history of Western thought and culture (rooted in Christianity, exacerbated by Descartes) and ushered in such notions as the 'embodied mind' and/or the 'mindful body' (Howes 2022a: 4, 35). This fusion represented an important correction, but it failed to address the situatedness of

---

[38] Other examples of this genre include my own analysis of the sense lives of Freud and Marx in *Sensual Relations* (Howes 2003: chs. 7 and 8), Classen's sensory biographies of Hildegard of Bingen, Jakob Boehme and Charles Fourier in *The Color of Angels* (Classen 1998: ch. 1) and Mark M. Smith's sensory profile of Abraham Lincoln in *A Sensory History Manifesto* (Smith 2021). See further 'Double conversion: A sensory autobiography of Sir Kenelm Digby' (Moshenska 2022): Digby was a contemporary and moved in the same circle as Margaret Cavendish.

[39] Whistler's *japonisme* was primarily mediated by these objects (he was an avid collector, who also decorated his succession of houses with oriental colour schemes and motifs), rather than by books. His conversations with other connoisseurs, such as Comte de Montesquiou (who gifted the Whistlers a pair of bonsai trees), probably influenced him as well (see Sutherland 2014: 57, 83–5; Willsdon 2018: 85–7).

the mind-body in a particular environment or historical context. The concept of emplacement does this by shifting the onus onto 'the sensuous interrelationship of body-mind-environment' (Howes 2005: 7) in addition to foregrounding the relations among the senses.

That said, it is challenging to apply the concept of emplacement to Whistler's self-fashioning, since his life consisted in a series of displacements. He was born in Lowell, Massachusetts in 1834, but the Whistler family moved to St. Petersburg in 1842 so his father, an engineer, could take up a commission offered him by Nicholas I of Russia to engineer a railroad from St. Petersburg to Moscow. After the father succumbed to cholera and died in 1849, the mother took her two young sons back to the States. Whistler gained admission (thanks to family connections) to West Point military academy, though he never did graduate (he was expelled for 'deficiencies' in chemistry in 1854). He then spent a short period at the US Coast and Geodetic Survey, in Washington, DC, where he trained in etching, which became the basis of his early career.

In 1855, Whistler quit the US to study art in Paris, and then in 1859 decamped to London. He would go on flitting back and forth between London and Paris throughout his artistic career, and so was very much a cosmopolitan individual or 'public man' – that is, one who 'moves comfortably in diversity' (Sennett 1977). He also made sorties to, among other places, Chile in 1866, Venice in 1879–80, Amsterdam in 1889, and went on an imaginary voyage to Japan, mediated by his collection of orientalia (mainly porcelain and prints).

Provocatively, in his testimony at the notorious 1878 libel trial (on which more later), Whistler claimed that he was born in St. Petersburg. When questioned about this, since he was actually born in the States, he responded: 'I shall be born when and where I want, and I do not choose to be born in Lowell, Massachusetts' (quoted in Peters 1996: 11; Sutherland 2014: 325). So, Whistler had no one place, not even a place of birth. He was always out of place and, I want to suggest, this constant *displacement* contributed substantially to his unique perspective on the world. The constant change in setting continuously renewed his perception, as it did the circle of his interlocutors.

In what follows, reference will be made to a wide assortment of Whistler's paintings and some of his lithographs, all of which are easily accessed via the reader's preferred Internet search engine. It is strongly recommended that the reader take the time to augment their reading of the text in this way.

Consider the trip to Chile. Whistler's biographers are uncertain about his motivation for suddenly upping and leaving London for Valparaiso in 1866, abandoning his mother and his mistress. He stayed away for close to seven months. Was it because he could not handle the tension between the women in his life: the live-in mistress, Joanna Hiffernan, and the strict Presbyterian mother, Anna McNeill Whistler (whose arrival in London in 1864 meant that Whistler had to arrange different lodgings for Hiffernan).[40] Or was it because he felt compelled to go and join with the Chileans in their liberation struggle against the Spanish? [41]

It was during his sojourn in Valparaiso that Whistler commenced his first 'moonlight', as he called them – *Nocturne in Blue and Gold: Valparaiso* (reworked in 1874). This painting depicts a harbour scene by the light of the moon in a blue and green palette flecked with bright dots. The quality of the light in South America is different from that in Europe, such as, for example, the bright light of the French-Italian Riviera that inspired Claude Monet, or the vaporous atmosphere of Venice that so fascinated J. M. W. Turner and others, as well as North America, where a distinctly American school of painting known as Luminism emerged in the 1850s.[42] Many painters are drawn to light. What was singular about Whistler is that he sought to capture the moonlight. It was the displacement to South America that opened his eyes.

Whistler's epiphany in Chile was as momentous an event as regards his artistic development as, say, the afternoons Picasso whiled away at the Musée Trocadero contemplating the African masks in the museum's collection. It is an interesting question whether Picasso would ever have been able to break with the tradition of linear perspective, and invent the multiperspectival vision on display in the works from his 'Cubist' period, such as *Les Demoiselles d'Avignon* (1907), had it not been for his exposure to the 'distorted features' of the masks (Rubin 1984). In any event, my point is this: the deepest artistic

---

[40] The mother came to London in 1864 to visit her son and his half-sister, Deborah Haden, and ended up moving in with Whistler for a protracted period. It is interesting to speculate on the influence Anna McNeill Whistler had on the formation of her son's character. The mother, being a very pious Presbyterian, was responsible for instilling in Whistler a strong work ethic, which explains his extraordinary productivity. At the same time, she doted on her 'Jimmy', and indulged him, which may explain his moral laxness (the succession of mistresses, the numerous illegitimate children). This contradiction came to a head in the way he worked industriously in his studio yet presented himself in public as an 'idler', who 'knocked off' his paintings in no time; as Whistler himself professed, 'the artist's only positive virtue is idleness – and there are so few who are gifted at it' (quoted in Anderson and Koval 1995: 219, 228). So, Whistler was a Bohemian Presbyterian, a product of his mother's strictness and indulgence at once.

[41] A third explanation is that Whistler went to Chile on business (Sutherland 2014: 95–8), but this explanation lacks the romance of the other two.

[42] The 2004 *Turner, Whistler, Monet: Impressionist Visions* exhibition (Lochnan 2004) at Tate Britain and the 1980 *American Light: The Luminist Movement, 1825–1875* exhibition (Wilmerding 1989) at the National Gallery of Art in Washington, DC. Interestingly, according to Whistler's mentor, Thomas Way, the preparatory studies the artist did for the nocturnes he painted in the 1880s consisted of 'sketches drawn in the dark, by feeling not by sight' (quoted in McNamara and Siewert 1994: 73). It appears that Whistler frequently engaged his neighbours the Greaves (father and brothers) to row him up and down the Thames across from his house in Chelsea all through the night hours so he could sketch (Sutherland 2014: 101; see further Willsdon 2018: 106–9; de Montfort 2013).

inspiration does not come from within; rather, it comes from crossing borders – from displacement in space, in Whistler's case.

If it is difficult to place Whistler geographically, it is no less challenging to situate him and his art sensorially. For example, he is famous for using musical phraseology, such as 'nocturne' and 'symphony', in the titles of his paintings. Indeed, one possible explanation for why many of Whistler's canvases appear so ethereal or abstract is that music was 'in the air', especially in fine art circles. As the essayist and critic Walter Pater proclaimed: 'All art constantly aspires towards the condition of music' (it being the most intangible and therefore transcendent medium of expression) and many artists, especially the Symbolists and the Impressionists, sought to hypostatize Pater's vision (quoted in Classen 2014c: 191; see further Classen 2014c: 173–81 and 1998: ch. 5; Bendix 1995: 40–2). This raises the question: Did Whistler put nature to music? Or, to approach this another way: Are Whistler's paintings about crossing senses, about 'seeing musically', as it were? [43]

Whistler actually credited his patron Frederick Leyland (a devotee of Chopin) for his musically inflected titles: 'I say', he wrote to Leyland, 'I can't thank you too much for the name "Nocturne" as a title for my moonlights! You have no idea what an irritation it proves to the critics and consequent pleasure to me – besides it is really so charming and does so poetically say all that I want to say and no more than I wish' (cited in Anderson and Koval 1995: 186). This suggests that music was more an idiom than it was the matrix of his art. He liked the way the musical analogy confounded his critics, but it must also have helped the public get a handle on what he was doing ('Oh, well, it makes sense when you put it that way . . .'). While obviously aiding the reception of his work, the question remains: What about the production? Did Whistler see musically?

Here, I take my cue from Clare Willsdon's paper entitled 'Sounding the garden: Whistler, Darwin and music' (Willsdon 2019a), which she presented at the 'Whistler, Nature and Science' study day at the Fitzwilliam Museum, Cambridge in 2019 (see further Willsdon 2019b). Her paper is exemplary of the new *multimodal* approach to art history, with its accent on intersensoriality.[44] It centres on the lithographs Whistler printed when he and his wife Beatrix lived at no. 110 Rue du Bac in Paris during the 1890s. Somewhat enigmatically, Whistler called his lithographs 'songs on stone'. The circumstances of their

---

[43] This issue has been imaginatively explored by John Siewert 2004 and Arabella Teniswood-Harvey 2006.

[44] The new multi/intersensory art history is keyed to the study of the separation, combination and interaction of the full gamut of senses (and corresponding media) in the production and reception of art. See, for example, Classen 1998 and 2014c; Jones 2006; Candlin 2010; Lauwrens 2012 and 2019; Shaw-Miller 2013; Deutsch 2021; Eberhart 2021; Dimova 2024; and Howes 2022a: chs. 6 and 8.

creation were certainly very sonorous. Beatrix kept numerous birds in cages, as can be seen in the print 'Beatrix Looking at Her Birds' (ca. 1893–5) and bird calls had recently come to be perceived as music, thanks to Darwin, Willsdon notes. Furthermore, the Whistlers' garden was adjacent to the seminary of the Société des Missions Étrangères de Paris, and we know that Whistler loved to go and sit on a bench in the garden and listen to the missionaries chanting. The chants were composed by Charles Gounod, perhaps the most famous one being *Le départ des missionaires*.

In line with these ideas and observations, Willsdon (2019a) suggests that we should approach Whistler's prints as musical compositions transposed onto lithographic plates, and when we contemplate the prints we should be able to not only hear the music but also see the colour. To elaborate: 'Gounod was praised for the expressive colour of his music. Saint-Saens even cast him as a painter, extolling his quest for "a beautiful colour on the orchestral palette"' (Willsdon 2019a: n.p.). Note how this is an inversion of Pater's dictum: evidently, the inspiration could flow both ways. Willsdon continues:

> We should remember that Erasmus Darwin proposed parallels between colours and musical notes and Whistler had pursued this idea with his symphonies and harmonies in paint.
>
> But Whistler now argued at Rue de Bac that the subtle lines of the lithograph ... conjured colour in themselves and were thus expressive. So the little delicate edges and soft touches and so on that he explored with lithography were ways to evoke colour even though he is using black and white. (Willsdon 2019a: n.p.; see further Willsdon 2018: 98–100)

As we are beginning to see, Whistler crossed geographic borders perpetually, and he also crossed perceptual borders by mingling music and lithography ('songs on stone'), music and painting (the 'nocturnes' and 'symphonies'). I propose that of particular significance to the development of his style was that he also crossed cultural borders in his artistic practice. Consider Whistler's imaginary sojourn in Japan. He never actually went to the East, but he was an avid (and discerning) collector of Chinese porcelain and Japanese prints, and counted Lafcadio Hearn, the famous chronicler of Japan, among his acquaintances and most frequent correspondents (Evangelista 2016).

At first, Whistler just depicted the things of Japanese culture, such as fans, kimonos and blue-and-white porcelain, as can be seen in *Purple and Rose: The Lange Lijzen of the Six Marks* (1864). This is not a very good painting. The artist approaches these orientalia more as a collector than a painter, and the atmosphere is more like that of a Victorian parlour (stuffy, chock-full of things) than a Japanese interior (best known for emptiness and minimalist décor). In time, however, Whistler attuned himself to Japanese aesthetics – that is, to Japanese ways of seeing – and expressed these Eastern techniques of perception in his paintings. Among other works, this altered vision finds expression in *Variations in Flesh Colour and Green: The Balcony* (1864/79) where we can see a cluster of European women dressed in Japanese apparel in the foreground and, on the other side of the expanse of water, a slagheap. The slagheaps and the general plan of the painting bear a striking resemblance to *Sazai Hall at the Temple of the Five Hundred Arhats (Gohyaku Rakanji Sazaidō)*, from the series *Thirty-Six Views of Mount Fuji* by Katsushika Hokusai (Dorment and Macdonald 1994: 85–9; Roeder 2021). In other words, Whistler has transposed Mount Fuji and Hokusai's aesthetic into the heart of England, specifically the London dockland.

Nocturne: Blue and Silver – Chelsea (1871) has a similar composition and could be seen as Japanese in style even though there are no Japanese things in this painting, only expanses, only intervals. It is precisely this expanse that makes the painting so Japanese. The interval, called *ma*, is very important in Japanese culture. *Ma* means 'gap'. The concept of the interval is both spatial and temporal. It is the instant between two notes in a piece of music, or the space between the figures in a painting. This area, left empty, is no less important than the areas that are filled in, for without this in-between there could be nothing, at least nothing that stands out. As Tomie Hahn (2007: 53) observes: '*Ma* is a particularly Japanese aesthetic where aspects of "negative" space and time are not believed to be empty but are considered to be expansive and full of energy.'

There is a theory of the Japanese way of sensing and how it differs from Western habits of perception.[45] It goes as follows: The Western mind, or 'gaze',

---

[45] The theory derives in part from William Caudill's classic study of Japanese vs. North American child-rearing practices: the emphasis on nonverbal communication and physical intimacy (mother–child communion) in the Japanese context is generative of a sociocentric or relational self, whereas the stress on verbal communication, assertiveness training and physical separation (the child in its crib) in the North American context produces an egocentric, bounded self or 'individual' (Caudill and Weinstein 1969). Other studies, such as those by Diana Tahhan (2015) on Japanese tactility and Inge Daniels (2010) on the Japanese interior, support this theory. Its import was brought home to me personally during a two-week visit to Tokyo in 2011, where I gave a course of lectures at the invitation of Professor Keizo Miyasaka of Keio University. Professor Miyasaka brought numerous little details to my attention, like the fact that no two high-rise towers may abut their whole height – there must remain a space (according to the building code in Tokyo) by way of illustration of the concept *ma*. He otherwise introduced me to the finer points of Japanese etiquette, kabuki theatre and what the Japanese see in the works of Paul Klee (there was a Klee exhibition on at MOMAT (National Museum of Modern Art, Tokyo) at the time). Professor Miyasaka also arranged for the two of us to go on a day trip to Kanagawa Prefecture to see the Great Buddha of Kamakura. The Buddha is situated in the grounds of the Kōtuku-in temple, and Professor Miyasaka's colleague, the archaeologist Takao Sato, is the head priest of the temple. We were supposed to go to tea in the traditional Japanese home of Professor Sato (situated adjacent to the temple), but he was called away, and so it was his mother, Michiko Sato, who received us, ever so graciously. We dined on corn on the cob and matcha ice cream and drank tea while seated on tatami mats at a sunken table in the middle of the living room, and

centres on things. As the phenomenologists tell us, consciousness is always 'consciousness *of* something'. By contrast, the Japanese gaze focusses on the in-between, and objects occupy the periphery of consciousness. Thus, the Japanese gaze is relational or interstitial, whereas the Western sensorium is thing-ful (from *res*, 'thing', which is also the root of the word 'real'), reificatory or realist, by and large. Have another look at *Nocturne: Blue and Silver – Chelsea*. Note the barge in the foreground and the factories on the distant shore with the 'empty' space of the river (which is actually quite charged) in between. Whistler has captured a very Japanese way of perceiving in this painting.[46]

If we cannot very well locate Whistler geographically or sensorially, can we locate him stylistically? The critic John Ruskin didn't think so. In his review of an exhibition at the Grosvenor Gallery which featured paintings by Burne-Jones (whom Ruskin admired overly much) and Whistler's ca. 1875 painting *Nocturne in Black and Gold: The Falling Rocket* (which is in the same vein as *Nocturne in Blue and Gold: Valparaiso*), the critic referred to the artist as 'a coxcomb', accused him of 'flinging a pot of paint in the public's face' and charging 200 guineas for it to boot (Sutherland 2014: 146; Anderson and Koval 1995: 215–27). Whistler brought a libel case against Ruskin for his effrontery.

The suggestion that Whistler was a 'coxcomb' was not really libel or slander. It was quite apt (*pace* Whistler). By definition, a coxcomb is 'a vain and conceited man'. Another term for suchlike is 'dandy'. In point of fact, not only was Whistler a dandy himself (the floppy hats, the flamboyant attire) but he also painted one of the greatest dandies of all time in his *Arrangement in Black and Gold: Comte Robert de Montesquiou-Fezensac* (1892).

Dandies have a bad reputation in Western culture. They are associated with decadence, the decline of civilization, decay and so on, and what is worse, according to their detractors, they dress up. 'Clothes make the man', they say, whereas right-minded men and women know this is not true: virtue comes from within, it is a question of mettle! The dandy tends toward dissipation. Only

---

gazed out over the traditional Japanese garden through the floor-to-ceiling picture window while chatting. The whole affair was ever so simple, supremely serene, and it brought home many points to me; for example, the seating arrangement gave me a direct experience of the low vantage point typical of Japanese painting. It is of ethnological interest to note that the majestic (13 metres tall) statue of the Buddha of Kamakura is no less wondrous on the inside (the bronze cast is hollow, of course). For a fee, one can enter through a narrow doorway at the base and climb up to be inside the Buddha's head. There is literally nothing there (but air), which makes for a truly zen experience.

[46] The fascination with margins that Willsdon (2018) discerns in Whistler's *oeuvre* may also be interpreted in terms of this theory of the relational gaze (see further de Montfort and Willsdon 2018). Other random observations can be assimilated to it as well, such as when Prideaux (1970: 12) notes: 'In this difficult medium [referring to etching] Whistler proved a master of omission, so refining his skill that what was left out became as important as what was left in . . . he knew how to make an unfilled space convey mood and atmosphere.' Think *ma*.

recently has the moralizing stigma attached to dandyism come to be questioned and the figure of the dandy to be repositioned as often in the vanguard of progressive social change.[47] Another thing about dandies that cannot be denied is that, whatever their (alleged) moral faults, their senses are exquisite. Think of Comte de Montesquiou, 'the quintessential aesthete', who was known as the 'Master of Delicate Odours', as well as the fictional character modelled after him – namely, Des Esseintes in J.-K. Huysmans' *Against Nature* (Classen 1998: 113–14; see further Willsdon 2018: 85–7).

Ruskin's allegation that Whistler 'flung a pot of paint in the public's face' puts me in mind of Norman Rockwell's *The Connoisseur* (1961). In this painting, Rockwell (mockingly?) depicts a pudgy man in a rumpled grey suit trying to fathom what appears to be a Jackson Pollock 'action painting', full of splattered paint. It would seem that in *The Connoisseur* Rockwell is giving the avant-garde artists of his day – namely, the Abstract Expressionists – a poke in the eye possibly in retaliation for the way the art world dismissed his paintings as mere illustrations. One senses that Rockwell would have been on the side of the man in the grey suit.[48] So too may Ruskin be identified with the befuddled spectator: he too was suspicious or even aghast at the direction 'modern art' was taking by this late stage in his otherwise eminently distinguished and colourful career (Ribeyrol et al. 2023).

Of course, this parallel is a complete anachronism from the viewpoint of conventional art history. But the very anachronism illustrates the larger point I'd like to make, which goes to Whistler's artistic style. As Tom Prideaux (1970: 11–12) writes: 'After his student apprenticeship in 19th Century Paris, he veered toward Realism, then toward the poetic idealism of the Pre-Raphaelites and next toward Impressionism.' In time, as a corollary to his advocacy of 'Art for Art's Sake' (see Sutherland 2014: 111, 143–4, 207–8), Prideaux (1970: 12) continues, Whistler 'increasingly tended toward abstract art', which made him 'a prophet well ahead of his time'. Prideaux's remarks do not actually give us the whole picture, though. Whistler himself professed that he was influenced by the painters of the Dutch and Spanish Baroque (Rembrandt, Velázquez). Thus, he was always *après* and *avant la lettre* at once. Whistler was a 'weathervane' (Prideaux 1970), a crossroads, or one could even say a 'hinge'. It bears

---

[47] Have a listen to Pedro Mendes' 'The Dandy Rebels' in the archives of the CBC Ideas program (see www.cbc.ca/listen/live-radio/1-23-ideas/clip/15837414-the-dandy-rebel). See further Curry 1984: 83–4.

[48] Received wisdom has it that the man in the grey suit might be smiling approvingly, and that Rockwell held Pollock and company in high regard. I beg to differ, while acknowledging that Rockwell was a more complex figure than he is typically given credit for (see http://canadiani con.org/table-of-contents/alex-colville-doing-justice-to-reality/).

noting that in addition to being a – or, perhaps, *the* – hinge of Western art, Whistler not infrequently came unhinged, flying off the handle and slapping or engaging in fisticuffs with people at the slightest provocation (Sutherland 2014: 73–4, 97–8, 103–4, 106–7).

One of Whistler's creations that particularly invites and merits scrutiny from our sensory biography of things perspective is *Blue and Silver: Screen, with the Old Battersea Bridge* (1871–2). I had the chance to witness this work, which is both an *objet d'art* and a stunning example of craftwork,[49] when I participated in a three-day workshop sponsored by the Aesthetic Network at the University of Glasgow in September 2016, which included a visit to the Hunterian Art Gallery.[50] My experience of this hinged artifact (significant, in view of the preceding discussion) was deeply influenced by my conversation with another participant in the workshop, the sensory anthropologist Rupert Cox, who is also a Japanologist of distinction.

In the Whistler Gallery at the Hunterian, the screen is free-standing and partially unfolded, not affixed to a wall, as it was for the longest time. It is a credit to the curators that they thought to display it this way, even if they also isolated it in a glass case. As Cox observes, the structure of the screen is analogous to a picture frame. It sets off the image on its surface as art. But the screen also has a function in everyday life. It is not just 'Art for art's sake'. It can be employed to divide up a room and divide up the people in a room – that is, it can be used as a backdrop (see Figure 2) or to create an alcove (frame a group of people as a conversation group and offer a topic for conversation).[51] The screen is therefore 'performative' in the sense that it partially encloses the viewer, or as Cox put it, the screen is 'a hybrid, mobile object, creating its own conditions for viewing, in the situations of its unfolding' (Cox in Howes et al. 2018: 330).

There is a further sense in which Whistler's screen is a 'mobile object'. It had travelled from Japan to Europe. As Cox notes, Japanese artists painted scenes of their encounters with Europeans on folding screens (*Byōbu*) such as this. The screens thus gave expression to a Japanese way of seeing European travellers. Whistler reversed this gaze by painting an image of Old Battersea Bridge over the original design (which was by the female Japanese artist Nampo Jhoshi).

---

[49] On the craft of making these folding screens (*Byōbu*), see Cox in Howes et al. 2018: 329–31.

[50] The Aesthetic Network was directed by Dee Reynolds and Boris Wiseman. Reynolds and Wiseman (2018) also edited a special issue of *The Senses and Society* on methods of aesthetic enquiry across disciplines.

[51] Significantly, Whistler loved to arrange people, both at social gatherings and in his paintings, Willsdon (2018) observes.

Figure 2 Whistler in his studio on the rue Notre-Dame-des-Champs,
Paris, 1893.

Source: Photo credit Paul François Arnold Cardon (called 'Dornac'), Yale Center for
British Art.

Somewhat anachronistically, but in keeping with the refusal of chronology
that we have seen to be one of Whistler's most distinctive traits, Cox proposes
that in its 'mobile visuality' and 'imaginative space for audio-vision' (that is, for
viewing and conversation), Whistler's screen 'anticipates ... the world of
screen-based media that we carry with us today, with images that flicker and
are swiped rather than unfolded' (Cox in Howes et al. 2018: 332). It is like
a house of mirrors (or a switchboard for the renvoi of glances East and West)
and at the same time an acoustic alcove – or, to put a finer point on it, the screen
that is also a painting both embodies and unfolds a bundle of intersensory,
interpersonal and intercultural relations.

In my research for the talk I gave at the 'Whistler, Nature and Industry'
symposium in 2021, organized by Clare Willsdon and Patricia de Montfort,
I came across a passage relating how Whistler's first solo show, in 1874, was
lauded for the design and decoration of the hall in which it was staged. This
harmonized well with the paintings. As the reviewer for *Pictorial World*, Henry
Blackburn, wrote:

> The visitor is struck, on entering the Gallery, with a curious sense of harmony and fitness pervading it, and is more interested, perhaps, in the general effect than in any one work. The Gallery and its contents are altogether in harmony – a symphony in colour, carried out, in every detail, even in the colour of the matted floor, the blue pots and flowering plants, and, above all, in the juxtaposition of the pictures. (cited in Anderson and Koval 1995: 197)[52]

To speak of 'the general effect' is to speak of the *atmosphere* of a space, rather than the space itself. Atmospheres are enveloping (Böhme 2017). Being arranged in the way Whistler arranged them for this show, the paintings do not stop at the edge of the canvas; rather, their colour schemes pervade the whole setting. This echoes the immersive effect of the paintings themselves: they do not depict landscapes (whether natural, industrial or in ruins) the way our 'thing-ful' eyes obstinately see them; they evoke atmospheres. Whistler was a painter of atmospheres, not of scenes. Furthermore, in his portraits of human subjects, the colour scheme is as important as the sitter. For example, in the case of the portrait Whistler did of his mother, the painting is entitled *Arrangement in Black and Grey No. 1: Portrait of the Artist's Mother* (1871). This decentring of the subject and the emphasis on harmonization (of colours as of people) is also very Japanese. As we have seen, the Japanese self is relational to the same degree the Western self is bounded and individualistic.

This section has shown how Whistler crossed borders (both geographical and cultural), crossed artistic styles and crossed the senses in his artistic practice. This mingling is the secret of his genius. He was the epitome of the cosmopolitan individual or 'public man' who 'moves comfortably in diversity' (Sennett 1977) and the paragon of the bricoleur (Lévi-Strauss 2020) in the way he mixed styles and pigments. He *symphonized* the senses, cultures and different spaces in his works. It agrees with the sensory biography of Whistler's *oeuvre* offered here that he has no one place in the history of Western art, and that his influence is everywhere.

Epilogue: Ways of Sensing

'Lead with the senses!' That is the rallying call of the 'sensorial revolution' in the humanities and social sciences that has been steadily gaining momentum over the past three decades (Howes 2022a). As more and more historians and anthropologists, geographers and sociologists (among others) have signed on, and the cross-disciplinary field of sensory studies has taken on definition (Bull

---

[52] See further *Mr. Whistler's Gallery* (Myers 2003). Much the same could be said of Whistler's makeover of the Peacock Room, commissioned (though not altogether appreciated) by Leyland and later acquired by the industrialist Charles Lang Freer (see generally Bendix 1995; Curry 1984).

et al. 2006), it has resulted in the toppling of the monopoly that the discipline of psychology (and its brainchild, cognitive neuroscience) formerly exercised over the study of perception and cognition. Psychology privatizes the senses and sense experience. This is particularly evident in the case of contemporary neuropsychology (the work of Ramachandran and company), which, continuing in the tradition of nineteenth-century psychophysics, focusses on the transmission of signals along the neural pathways from the sense organ (or 'transducer') to their terminus in the visual cortex, the auditory cortex, the rhinencephalon and so on. In this way, the senses have been made to retreat inside the head, and be subsumed by the brain.

There are those who would contest this subsumption, Margaret Lucas Cavendish being one. In her memorable phrase, 'The Heads Braines cannot ingross all knowledge to themselves' (quoted in Classen 1998: 101). As discussed in the prologue, Walter Ong also resisted this process of involution, and flipped it. In his seminal essay on 'The shifting sensorium' (1991), Ong 'outered' the senses by retrieving the archaic definition of the term 'sensorium' and redirecting attention to the enculturation of the senses. His approach helped sensitize us to how, in the ancient Greek as in the ancient Chinese and Indian conceptions of the universe, the divisions of the sensorium were isomorphic to those of the cosmos, and not just anatomical. This led us to recognize that the senses are our first media, and they are susceptible to a near infinite array of combinations and modulations. Ong's approach, augmented by taking into account Mauss' and Simmel's sociologies of the body and senses, also sensitized us to the degree to which perception is a matter of technique. This realization in turn informed our analysis of different ways of hearing, smelling and seeing feelingly in Sections 1, 2 and 3. Part I concluded with a discussion of Boaventura de Sousa Santos' clarion call – in *The End of the Cognitive Empire* (Santos 2018) – to attend to 'the crisscrossed multiplicity of the senses' across 'the abyssal line' (North/South, metropolitan/colonial, scientific/nonscientific) and, we would add, throughout history. The sensorium is a historical formation; there is no escaping the political life of sensation.

Part II offered a pair of *études sensorielles*: the first *étude* centred on the writer Margaret Lucas Cavendish's alternative sensuous epistemology, and the second presented a sensory biography of the painter James McNeill Whistler's works and life. 'Don't psychologize; contextualize!' was the watchword of these two case studies, and with their emphasis on the twin notions of emplacement and displacement, they opened our thinking to the plurality of possible ways of sensing, and the cognitive and aesthetic as well as the judicious and liberatory implications thereof. The lesson to be derived from our exploration of the works of Cavendish in Section 5, and the crossing of sensory, artistic and cultural borders in Whistler's *oeuvre* in Section 6, is that sensory critique is the beginning of cultural and epistemological critique, and that social as well as artistic transformation is conditional on sensory emancipation. *Vive la révolution sensorielle*!

References

Aagard, J. 2021. '4E cognition and the dogma of harmony', *Philosophical Psychology*, 34(2): 165–81.

Allen, J. 2008. 'The beautiful science', *Frieze Magazine*, 113 (March).

Anderson, R. and A. Koval. 1995. *James McNeill Whistler: Beyond the Myth* (New York: Carroll & Graf).

Appadurai, A., ed. 1986. *The Social Life of Things* (Cambridge: Cambridge University Press).

Aristotle. n.d. *De Anima* (*On the Soul*), *Classics in the History of Psychology*. https://psychclassics.yorku.ca/Aristotle/De-anima/de-anima3.htm.

Arnheim, R. 1969. *Visual Thinking* (Berkeley: University of California Press).

Art Education for the Blind. 1998–9. *Art History through Touch and Sound* (Louisville, KY: American Printing House for the Blind).

Barad, K. 2007. *Meeting the Universe Halfway: Quantum Physics and the Entanglement of Matter and Meaning* (Durham, NC: Duke University Press).

Baron-Cohen, S., M. A. Wyke and C. Binnie. 1987. 'Hearing words and seeing colours: An experimental investigation of a case of synaesthesia', *Perception*, 16: 761–7.

Basso, E. 1985. *A Musical View of the Universe: Kalapalo Myth and Ritual Performances* (Philadelphia: University of Pennsylvania Press).

Bateson, G. 1972. 'Style, grace and information in primitive art', in *Steps to an Ecology of Mind*, 128–52 (North Vale, NJ: Jason Aronson).

Bath, P., T. Girault and E. Waterman. 2023. 'Reflecting on *Bodily Listening in Place*: An intercultural and intersensory research-creation project', *Performance Matters*, 9(1–2): 139–54.

Battigelli, A. 1998. *Margaret Cavendish and the Exiles of the Mind* (Lexington: University Press of Kentucky).

Bedini, S. 1994. *The Trail of Time: Time Measurement with Incense in East Asia* (Cambridge: Cambridge University Press).

Bendix, D. M. 1995. *Diabolical Designs: Paintings, Interiors and Exhibitions of James McNeill Whistler* (Washington, DC: Smithsonian Institution Press).

Bendix, R. 2005. 'Time of the senses?', *Current Anthropology*, 45(4): 688–90.

Bennett, J. 2010. *Vibrant Matter: A Political Ecology of Things* (Durham, NC: Duke University Press).

Biddle, J. 2007. *Breasts, Bodies, Canvas: Central Desert Art as Experience* (Sydney: University of New South Wales Press).

Biddle, J. 2016. *Remote Avant-Garde: Aboriginal Art under Occupation* (Durham, NC: Duke University Press).

Blake, S. 2019. 'Perception and its disorders in early China', in *The Senses and the History of Philosophy*, B. Glenney and J. F. Silva, eds., 33–48 (Abingdon: Routledge).

Boddice, R. and M. Smith. 2020. *Emotion, Sense, Experience* (Cambridge: Cambridge University Press).

Böhme, G. 2017. *The Aesthetics of Atmospheres* (Abingdon: Routledge).

Bonin, E. L. 2009. 'Margaret Cavendish's dramatic utopias and the politics of gender', in *Ashgate Critical Essays on Women Writers in England, 1550–1700, Vol. 7: Margaret Cavendish*, S. H. Mendelson, ed., 115–30 (Farnham: Ashgate).

Bourdieu, P. 1984. *Distinction: A Social Critique of the Judgment of Taste* (Cambridge, MA: Harvard University Press).

Boyle, D. 2004. 'Margaret Cavendish's nonfeminist natural philosophy', *Configurations*, 12(2): 195–227.

Boyle, D. 2018. *The Well-Ordered Universe: The Philosophy of Margaret Cavendish* (Oxford: Oxford University Press).

Bruyninckx, J. 2023. 'An unquiet quiet: The history and "smart" politics of sound masking in the office', in *Techniques of Hearing: History, Theory and Practices*, M. Schillmeier, R. Stock and B. Ochsner, eds., 1–12 (Abingdon: Routledge).

Bull, M. 2000. *Sounding Out the City: Personal Stereos and the Management of Everyday Life* (Abingdon: Routledge).

Bull, M. 2007. *Sound Moves: iPod Culture and Urban Experience* (Abingdon: Routledge).

Bull, M., P. Gilroy, D. Howes and D. Kahn. 2006. 'Introducing sensory studies', *The Senses and Society*, 1(1): 3–7.

Burnett, C., M. Fend and P. Gouk, eds. 1991. *The Second Sense: Studies in Hearing and Musical Judgment from Antiquity to the Seventeenth Century* (London: Warburg Institute).

Calvert, G., C. Spence and B. Stein, eds. 2004. *The Handbook of Multisensory Processes* (Cambridge, MA: MIT Press).

Candlin, F. 2010. *Art, Museums and Touch* (Manchester: Manchester University Press).

Canévet, M., P. Adnès, W. Yeomans and A. Derville. 1993. *Les sens spirituels* (Paris: Beauchesne).

Casini, S. 2021. *Giving Bodies Back to Data* (Cambridge, MA: MIT Press).

Caudill, W. and H. Weinstein. 1969. 'Maternal care and infant behavior in Japan and America', *Psychiatry*, 32(1): 12–43.

Cavendish, M. 1653. *Poems, and Fancies.* (n.p.: Proquest Early English Books Online).

Cavendish, M. [1664a] 1997. *Margaret Cavendish: Sociable Letters*, J. Fitzmaurice, ed. (London: Garland Publishing).

Cavendish, M. 1664b. *Philosophical Letters.* (n.p.: Proquest Early English Books Online).

Cavendish, M. [1666a] 2001. *Observations upon Experimental Philosophy* (Cambridge: Cambridge University Press).

Cavendish, M. [1666b] 2016. *A Description of the Blazing World*, S. H. Mendelson, ed. (Peterborough: Broadview Editions).

Cavendish, M. [1668] 1999. *The Convent of Pleasure and Other Plays*, A. Shaver, ed. (Baltimore, MD: Johns Hopkins University Press).

Çelik, Z. 2006. 'Kinaesthesia', in *Sensorium*, C. A. Jones, ed., 159–62 (Cambridge, MA: MIT Press).

Chao, S., K. Bolender and E. Kirksey, eds. 2022.*The Promise of Multispecies Justice* (Durham, NC: Duke University Press).

Chapman, G. [1595] 2014. *Ovid's Banquet of Sense*, A. C. Swinburne, intro. (London: Pelta Books). Note that the original work had the spelling 'Sence' but the 2014 edition has adopted the modern spelling.

Chemero, A. 2009. *Radical Embodied Cognitive Science* (Cambridge, MA: MIT Press).

Clarke, A. 2008. *Supersizing the Mind: Embodiment, Action and Cognitive Extension* (Oxford: Oxford University Press).

Classen, C. [1993a] 2023. *Worlds of Sense* (London: Routledge).

Classen, C. 1993b. *Inca Cosmology and the Human Body* (Salt Lake City: University of Utah Press).

Classen, C. 1997. 'Foundations for an anthropology of the senses', *International Social Science Journal*, 153: 401–12.

Classen C. 1998. *The Color of Angels: Cosmology, Gender and the Aesthetic Imagination* (London: Routledge).

Classen, C. 2001. 'The senses', in *Encyclopedia of European Social History from 1350 to 2000, Vol. 4*, P. Stearns, ed. (New York: Charles Scribner's Sons).

Classen, C. 2005. 'The witch's senses: Sensory ideologies and transgressive femininities from the Renaissance to Modernity', in *Empire of the Senses*, D. Howes, ed., 70–84 (Abingdon: Routledge).

Classen, C. 2007. 'Museum manners: The sensory life of the early museum', *Journal of Social History*, 40(4): 895–914.

Classen, C., ed. 2014a. *A Cultural History of the Senses*, 6 vols. (London: Bloomsbury).

Classen, C., ed. 2014b. *A Cultural History of the Senses in the Age of Empire, 1800–1920*, Vol. 5 of *A Cultural History of the Senses*, 6 vols., C. Classen, ed. (London: Bloomsbury).

Classen, C. 2014c. 'Art and the senses: From the Romantics to the Futurists', in *A Cultural History of the Senses in the Age of Empire, 1800–1920*, C. Classen, ed., 185–210 (London: Bloomsbury).

Classen, C. 2017. *The Museum of the Senses: Experiencing Art and Collections* (London: Bloomsbury).

Classen, C. 2020. 'The senses at the National Gallery: Art as sensory recreation and regulation in Victorian England', *The Senses and Society*, 15(1): 85–97.

Classen, C. 2023. 'Sensitive ecology', paper presented at the Uncommon Senses IV conference, Concordia University, Montreal, 3–6 May.

Classen, C., D. Howes and A. Synnott. 1994. *Aroma: The Cultural History of Smell* (London: Routledge).

Clucas, S. 2022. 'Margaret Cavendish and rhetoric and aesthetics of the microscopic image in seventeenth-century England', in *Margaret Cavendish: An Interdisciplinary Perspective*, L. Walters and B. R. Siegfried, eds., 51–68 (Cambridge: Cambridge University Press).

Connor, S. 2006. 'The menagerie of the senses', *The Senses and Society*, 1(1): 9–26.

Connor, S. 2015. 'Literature, technology and the senses', in *The Cambridge Companion to the Body in Literature*, D. Hillman and U. Maude, eds., 177–96 (Cambridge: Cambridge University Press).

Corbin, A. 1986. *The Foul and the Fragrant: Odor and the French Social Imagination* (Cambridge, MA: Harvard University Press).

Corbin, A. 1998. *Village Bells: Sound and Meaning in the Nineteenth-Century French Countryside* (New York: Columbia University Press).

Csordas, T. 1990. 'Embodiment as a paradigm for anthropology', *Ethos*, 18(1): 5–47.

Cunning, D. 2022. 'Cavendish, *Philosophical Letters* and the plenum', in *Margaret Cavendish: An Interdisciplinary Perspective*, L. Walters and B. R. Siegfried, eds., 98–111 (Cambridge: Cambridge University Press).

Curry, D. P. 1984. *James McNeill Whistler at the Freer Gallery of Art* (New York: W. W. Norton & Co.).

Cytowic, R. 1998. *The Man Who Tasted Shapes* (Cambridge, MA: MIT Press).

Daniels, I. 2010. *The Japanese House: Material Culture in the Modern Home* (Abingdon: Routledge).

De Kerckhove, D. 1998. *La civilisation vidéo-chrétienne* (Paris: Éditions Retz).

de Montfort, P. 2013. 'Painting river pictures', in *An American in London: Whistler and the Thames*, M. Macdonald and P. de Montfort, eds. (London: Philip Wilson).

de Montfort, P. and C. Willsdon. 2018. *Whistler and Nature* (London: Paul Holberton).

Deroy, O. and C. Spence. 2013a. 'Why we are not all synesthetes (not even weakly so)', *Psychonomic Bulletin & Review*, 20(4): 643–64.

Deroy, O. and C. Spence. 2013b. 'Are we all born synaesthetic? Examining the neonatal synaesthesia hypothesis', *Neuroscience and Behavioral Reviews*, 37: 1240–53.

DeSalle, R. 2018. *Our Senses* (New Haven, CT: Yale University Press).

Desjarlais, R. 2003. *Sensory Biographies* (Berkeley: University of California Press).

Deutsch, A. 2021. *Consuming Painting: Food and the Feminine in Impressionist Paris* (University Park: Pennsylvania State University Press).

Dimova. P. 2024. *At the Crossroads of the Senses: The Synaesthetic Metaphor Across the Arts in European Modernism*. University Park: Pennsylvania State University Press.

Dorment, R. and M. F. Macdonald. 1994. *James McNeill Whistler* (London: Tate).

Douglas, H. 2005. 'Customary law, sentencing and the limits of the state', *Canadian Journal of Law and Society*, 20(1): 141–56.

Dumit, J. 2004. *Picturing Personhood* (Princeton, NJ: Princeton University Press).

Dundas, J. 1985. '"To see feelingly": The language of the senses and the language of the heart', *Comparative Drama*, 19(1): 49–57.

Durie, B. 2005. 'Doors of perception', *New Scientist* (29 January), 185(2484): 34–6.

Eberhart, M. L. 2021. 'A web of sensation and the performance of memory: Dosso's lamenting Apollo', in *Embodiment, Expertise, and Ethics in Early Modern Europe: Entangling the Senses*, M. L. Eberhart and J. M. Brain, eds., 17–46 (Abingdon: Routledge).

Ehm, C., É. Pacherie, J.-D. Bagot, J. Dokic and R. Casati. 1999. *L'ABCdaire des cinq sens* (Paris: Flammarion).

Elkins, J. 2008. *How to Use Your Eyes* (New York: Routledge).

Eschenbaum, N. K. 2020. 'Robert Herrick and the five (or six) senses', in *The Senses in Early Modern England, 1558–1660*, S. Smith, J. Watson and A. Kenny, eds., 113–29 (Manchester: Manchester University Press).

Evangelista, S. 2016. 'Symphonies in haze and blue: Lafcadio Hearn and the colours of Japan', in *The Colours of the Past in Victorian England*, C. Ribeyrol, ed., 71–94 (Oxford: Peter Lang).

Fagan, J. J. and M. Tarabichi. 2018. 'Cochlear implants in developing countries: Practical and ethical considerations', *Current Opinion in Otolaryngology & Head and Neck Surgery*, 26(3): 188–9.

Farquhar, J. 2002. *Appetites: Food and Sex in Postsocialist China* (Durham, NC: Duke University Press).

Farquhar, J. 2020. *A Way of Life: Things, Thought and Action in Chinese Medicine* (New Haven, CT: Yale University Press).

Febvre, L. [1942] 1982. *The Problem of Unbelief in the Sixteenth Century* (Cambridge, MA: Harvard University Press).

Feld, S. [1982] 2012. *Sound and Sentiment: Birds, Weeping, Poetics and Song in Kaluli Expression* (Durham, NC: Duke University Press).

Feld, S. 1991a. 'Sound as a symbolic system: The Kaluli drum', in *The Varieties of Sensory Experience*, D. Howes, ed., 79–99 (Toronto: University of Toronto Press).

Feld, S. 1991b. *Voices of the Rainforest*. Washington, DC: Smithsonian Folk Ways recordings.

Feld, S. 2005. 'Places sensed, senses placed: Toward a sensuous epistemology of environments', in *Empire of the Senses*, D. Howes, ed., 179–91 (Abingdon: Routledge).

Feld, S. and A. Boudreault-Fournier. 2022. 'Sonic relations: Anthropology of/in sound – A conversation with Steven Feld', Sensory Studies. www.sensorystudies.org/sonic-relations/.

Fijn, N. and M. Kavesh, eds. 2021. 'Sense-making in a more-than-human world', *Australian Journal of Anthropology*, 32(1), special issue.

Foucault, M. 1977. *Discipline and Punish: The Birth of the Prison* (Harmondsworth: Penguin).

Fox Keller, E. and C. Grontkowski. 1983. 'The mind's eye', in *Discovering Reality*, S. Harding and M. Hintikka, eds., 207–24 (Dordrecht: Reidel).

Freud, S. 1953–74. *The Complete Psychological Works*, 24 vols. (London: Hogarth Press).

Friedner, M. 2022. *Sensory Futures: Deafness and Cochlear Implant Infrastructures in India* (Minneapolis: University of Minnesota Press).

Galton, F. 1894. 'Arithmetic by smell', *Psychological Review*, 1: 61–2.

Gavrilyuk, P. E. and S. Coakley, eds. 2011. *The Spiritual Senses* (Cambridge: Cambridge University Press).

Geaney, J. 2002. *On the Epistemology of the Senses in Early Chinese Thought* (Honolulu: University of Hawaii Press).

Geertz, C. 1983. *Local Knowledge* (Boston, MA: Beacon Books).

Geertz, C. 2001. 'The uses of diversity', in *Available Light* (Princeton, NJ: Princeton University Press).

Graif, P. 2018. *Being and Hearing: Making Intelligible Worlds in Deaf Kathmandu* (Chicago, IL: HAU Books/University of Chicago Press).

Gregor, M. J. 1983. 'Baumgarten's Aesthetika', *Review of Metaphysics*, 37: 367–85.

Gregory, R. L. 2015. *Eye and Brain: The Psychology of Seeing*, 5th ed. (Princeton, NJ: Princeton University Press).

Guru, G. and S. Sarukkai. 2019. *Experience, Caste and the Everyday Social* (Oxford: Oxford University Press).

Haffke, M. 2023. 'Adaptive environments: Ambient media and the temporalities of sonic self-care', in *Techniques of Hearing: History, Theory and Practices*, M. Schillmeier, R. Stock and B. Ochsner, eds., 139–50 (Abingdon: Routledge).

Hahn, T. 2007. *Sensational Knowledge: Embodying Culture Through Japanese Dance* (Middletown, CT: Wesleyan University Press).

Halpern, O. 2015. *Beautiful Data* (Durham, NC: Duke University Press).

Hamilakis, Y. 2014. *Archaeology and the Senses* (Cambridge: Cambridge University Press).

Haraway, D. 1988. 'Situated knowledges: The science question in feminism and the privilege of partial perspective', *Feminist Studies*, 14(3): 575–99.

Haraway, D. 2016. *Staying with the Trouble: Making Kin in the Chthulucene* (Durham, NC: Duke University Press).

Heller-Roazen, D. 2007. *The Inner Touch: Archaeology of a Sensation* (Cambridge, MA: Zone Books).

Heller-Roazen, D. 2008. 'Common sense: Greek, Arabic, Latin', in *Rethinking the Medieval Senses: Heritage, Fascinations, Frames*, S. G. Nichols, A. Kablitz and A. Calhoun, eds., 30–50 (Baltimore, MD: Johns Hopkins University Press).

Henderson, J. 1984. *The Development and Decline of Chinese Cosmology* (New York: Columbia University Press).

Higgins, H. B. 2014. 'Art and the senses: The avant-garde challenge to the visual arts', in *A Cultural History of the Senses in the Modern Age, 1920–2000*, D. Howes, ed., 195–218 (London: Bloomsbury).

Hooke, R. 1665. *Micrographia, or, Some Physiological Descriptions of Minute Bodies Made by Magnifying Glasses with Observations and Inquiries Thereupon* (London: James Allestry / Early English Books On-Line).

Howes, D. 1990. 'Les techniques des sens', *Anthropologie et Sociétés*, 14(2): 99–115.

Howes, D., ed. 1991. *The Varieties of Sensory Experience* (Toronto: University of Toronto Press).

Howes, D. 2003. *Sensual Relations* (Ann Arbor: University of Michigan Press).

Howes, D., ed. 2005. *Empire of the Senses* (Abingdon: Routledge).

Howes, D. 2006. 'Scent, sound and synaesthesia: Intersensoriality and material culture theory', in *Handbook of Material Culture*, C. Tilley, W. Keane, S. Küchler, M. Rowlands and P. Spyer, eds., 161–72 (London: Sage).

Howes, D. 2011. 'Hearing scents, tasting sights: Toward a cross-cultural multi-modal theory of aesthetics', in *Art and the Senses*, F. Bacci and D. Mellon, eds., 161–82 (Oxford: Oxford University Press).

Howes, D., ed. 2014. *A Cultural History of the Senses in the Modern Age, 1920–2000*, Vol. 6 of *A Cultural History of the Senses*, 6 vols., C. Classen, ed. (London: Bloomsbury).

Howes, D. 2018. 'The skinscape: Reflections on the dermalogical turn', *Body and Society* 24(1–2): 225–39.

Howes, D. 2020. 'Digging up the sensorium: On the sensory revolution in archaeology', in *The Routledge Handbook of Sensory Archaeology*, R. Skeates and J. Day, eds., 21–34 (Abingdon: Routledge).

Howes, D. 2022a. *The Sensory Studies Manifesto* (Toronto: University of Toronto Press).

Howes, D. 2022b. 'In defense of materiality: Attending to the sensori-social life of things', *Journal of Material Culture*, 27(3): 313–35.

Howes, D. 2023. *Sensorial Investigations* (University Park: Pennsylvania State University Press).

Howes D., E. Clarke, F. Macpherson, B. Best and R. Cox. 2018. 'Sensing art and artifacts', *The Senses and Society*, 13(3): 317–34.

Howes, D. and C. Classen. 2013. *Ways of Sensing* (Abingdon: Routledge).

Hull, J. M. 1992. *Touching the Rock: An Experience of Blindness* (New York: Penguin Random House).

Hutton, S. 2003. 'Science and satire', in *Authorial Conquests: Essays on Genre in the Writings of Margaret Cavendish*, L. Cottegnies and N. Weitz, eds., 161–78 (London: Associated University Presses).

Huysmans, J.-K. [1884] 1959. *Against Nature* (London: Penguin Classics).

Ingold, T. 2000. *The Perception of the Environment* (London: Routledge).

James, S. 2009. 'The philosophical innovations of Margaret Cavendish', in *Ashgate Critical Essays on Women Writers in England, 1550–1700, Vol. 7: Margaret Cavendish*, S. H. Mendelson, ed., 209–34 (Farnham: Ashgate).

Jay, M. 1993. *Downcast Eyes: The Denigration of Vision in Contemporary French Thought* (Berkeley: University of California Press).

Johnson, J. H. 1996. *Listening in Paris* (Berkeley: University of California Press).

Jones, C. A. 2005. *Eyesight Alone: Clement Greenberg's Modernism and the Bureaucratization of the Senses* (Chicago, IL: University of Chicago Press).

Jones, C. A., ed. 2006. S*ensorium: Embodied Experience, Technology and Contemporary Art* (Cambridge, MA: MIT Press).

Jones, C. A. 2018. 'The mediated sensorium', in *Senses and Sensation: Critical and Primary Sources, Vol. 4: Art and Design*, D. Howes, ed., 219–62 (Abingdon: Routledge).

Jones, C. A., R. Uchill and D. Mather. 2016. 'Preface', in *Experience: Culture, Cognition and the Common Sense*, C. A. Jones, R. Uchill and D. Mather, eds., 8–9 (Cambridge, MA: MIT Press).

Jordanova, L. 1989. *Sexual Visions* (New York: Harvester Wheatsheaf).

Jütte, R. 2005. *A History of the Senses* (Cambridge: Polity Press).

Kant, I. [1781] 1998. *Critique of Pure Reason* (Cambridge: Cambridge University Press).

Kant, I. 1978. *Anthropology from a Pragmatic Point of View* (Carbondale: Southern Illinois University Press).

Kearney, R. 1988. *The Wake of Imagination* (London: Routledge).

Keller, E. 2009. 'Producing petty gods: Margaret Cavendish's critique of experimental science', in *Ashgate Critical Essays on Women Writers in England, 1550–1700, Vol. 7: Margaret Cavendish*, S. H. Mendelson, ed., 171–96 (Farnham: Ashgate).

Kermode, F. 1971. 'The banquet of sense', in *Shakespeare, Spenser, Donne*, 84–115 (London: Routledge).

Kettler, A. 2021. 'Blinding lights and sensory others in Margaret Cavendish's Blazing World', in *Embodiment, Expertise and Ethics in Early Modern Europe: Entangling the Senses*, M. L. Eberhart and J. M. Baum, eds., 178–205 (Abingdon: Routledge).

Kirshenblatt-Gimblett, B. 1998. *Destination Culture* (Berkeley: University of California Press).

Klima, A. 2002. *The Funeral Casino* (Princeton, NJ: Princeton University Press).

Kopytoff, I. 1986. 'The cultural biography of things: Commoditization as process', in *The Social Life of Things*, A. Appadurai, ed., 64–92 (Cambridge: Cambridge University Press).

Lauwrens, J. 2012. 'Welcome to the revolution: The sensory turn and art history', *Journal of Art Historiography*, 7: 1–17.

Lauwrens, J. 2019. 'Seeing touch and touching sight: A reflection on the tactility of vision', *The Senses and Society*, 14(3): 297–312.

Leahy, H. R. 2012. *Museum Bodies: The Politics and Practices of Visiting and Viewing* (London: Routledge).

Levin, D. M., ed. 1993. *Modernity and the Hegemony of Vision* (Berkeley: University of California Press).

Lévi-Strauss, C. 2020. *Wild Thought: A New Translation of 'La pensée sauvage'* (Chicago, IL: University of Chicago Press).

Lévi-Strauss, C. and D. Eribon. 2018. 'Sensible qualities', in *Senses and Sensation: Critical and Primary Sources, Vol. 1: Anthropology and Geography*, D. Howes, ed., 39–42 (Abingdon: Routledge).

Lloyd, S. and A. Tremblay. 2021. '"No hearing without signals": Imagining and reimagining transductions through the history of the cochlear implant', *The Senses and Society*, 16(3): 259–77.

Lochnan, K. 2004. *Turner, Whistler, Monet: Impressionist Visions* (London: Tate Publishing).

Locke, J. [1689] 1975. *An Essay Concerning Human Understanding* (Oxford: Clarendon Press).

Mauss, M. [1936] 1979. *Sociology and Psychology Essays* (London: Routledge and Kegan Paul).

Mazzia, C. 2005. 'The senses divided: Organs, objects and media in early modern England', in *Empire of the Senses*, D. Howes, ed., 85–105 (Abingdon: Routledge).

McHugh, J. 2012. *Sandalwood and Carrion* (Oxford: Oxford University Press).

McLuhan, M. 1962. *The Gutenberg Galaxy* (Toronto: University of Toronto Press).

McLuhan, M. 1964. *Understanding Media* (New York: New American Library).

McLuhan, M. and Q. Fiore. 1967. *The Medium Is the Massage* (Harmondsworth: Penguin).

McNamara, C. and J. Siewert. 1994. *Whistler: Prosaic Views, Poetic Vision* (New York: Thames and Hudson).

Meade, M. S. and M. Emch. 2010. *Medical Geography* (New York: Guilford Press).

Merchant, C. 1980. *The Death of Nature: Women, Ecology and the Scientific Revolution* (San Francisco, CA: Harper and Row).

Merleau-Ponty, M. 1962. *Phenomenology of Perception* (London: Routledge & Kegan Paul).

Mollo, E., F. Boero, J. Peñuales, et al. 2022. 'Taste and smell: A unifying chemosensory theory', *Quarterly Review of Biology*, 97(2): 69–94.

Moshenska, J. 2022. 'Double conversion: A sensory autobiography of Sir Kenelm Digby', in *Sensing the Sacred in Medieval and Early Modern*

Culture, R. Macdonald, E. Murphy and E. Swann, eds., 81–98 (Abingdon: Routledge).

Myers, K. J. 2003. *Mr. Whistler's Gallery* (London: Scala Publishers).

Nate, R. 2009. '"Plain and vulgarly express'd": Margaret Cavendish and the discourse of the New Science', in *Ashgate Critical Essays on Women Writers in England, 1550–1700, Vol. 7: Margaret Cavendish*, S. H. Mendelson, ed., 235–50 (Farnham: Ashgate).

Newhauser, R., ed. 2014. *A Cultural History of the Senses in the Middle Ages, 500–1450*, Vol. 2 of *A Cultural History of the Senses*, 6 vols., C. Classen, ed. (London: Bloomsbury).

Noë, A. 2006. *Action in Perception* (Cambridge, MA: MIT Press).

O'Callaghan, C. 2019. *A Multisensory Philosophy of Perception* (Oxford: Oxford University Press).

Ochsner, B. and S. Miyazaki. 2023. 'The future is ear: Infrastructures of "smart hearing"', in *Techniques of Hearing: History, Theory and Practices*, M. Schillmeier, R. Stock and B. Ochsner, eds., 90–101 (Abingdon: Routledge).

Oliveros, P. 2005. *Deep Listening* (New York: iUniverse).

Ong, W. J. 1967. *The Presence of the Word* (New Haven, CT: Yale University Press).

Ong, W. J. 1991. 'The shifting sensorium', in *The Varieties of Sensory Experience*, D. Howes, ed., 25–30 (Toronto: University of Toronto Press).

Papenberg, J. G. 2023. 'Pleasure and pain with amplified sound: A sound and music history of loudspeaker systems in Germany, ca. 1930', in *Techniques of Hearing: History, Theory and Practices*, M. Schillmeier, R. Stock and B. Ochsner, eds., 36–46 (Abingdon: Routledge).

Paterson, M. 2021. *How We Became Sensorimotor* (Minneapolis: University of Minnesota Press).

Peters, L. 1996. *James McNeill Whistler* (New York: Smithmark).

Pohl, N. 2003. '"Of mixt natures": Questions of genre in Margaret Cavendish's *The Blazing World*', in *A Princely Brave Woman*, S. Clucas, ed., 51–68 (Aldershot: Ashgate).

Prideaux, T. 1970. *The World of Whistler, 1834–1903* (Boston, MA: Little, Brown and Company).

Proust, M. 1913–27. *À la recherche du temps perdu*, 7 vols. (Paris: Éditions Grasset).

Ramachandran, V. S., E. M. Hubbard and P. A. Butcher. 2004. 'Synesthesia, cross-activation, and the foundations of neuroepistemology', in *The Handbook of Multisensory Processes*, G. Calvert, C. Spence and B. Stein, eds., 867–83 (Cambridge, MA: MIT Press).

Rees, E. L. E. 2003. 'Triply bound: Genre and the exilic self', in *Authorial Conquests: Essays on Genre in the Writings of Margaret Cavendish*, L. Cottegnies and N. Weitz, eds., 23–39 (London: Associated University Presses).

Rennies, J. 2023. 'Better hearing for all: Smart solutions for the clinical, subclinical, and normal-hearing population', in *Techniques of Hearing: History, Theory and Practices*, M. Schillmeier, R. Stock and B. Ochsner, eds., 77–89 (Abingdon: Routledge).

Reynolds, D. and B. Wiseman, eds. 2018. 'Methods of aesthetic enquiry: Interdisciplinary encounters', *The Senses and Society*, 13(3), special issue.

Rhine, J. B. 1934. *Extra-Sensory Perception* (Boston, MA: Society for Psychic Research).

Ribeyrol, C., M. Winterbottom and M. Hewitson. 2023. *Colour Revolution: Victorian Art, Fashion and Design* (Oxford: Ashmolean Museum).

Ritchie, I. 1991. 'Fusion of the faculties', in *The Varieties of Sensory Experience*, D. Howes, ed. 192–202 (Toronto: University of Toronto Press).

Röder, B. and F. Rösler. 2004. 'Compensatory plasticity as a consequence of sensory loss', in *The Handbook of Multisensory Processes*, G. Calvert, C. Spence and B. Stein, eds., 719–48 (Cambridge, MA: MIT Press).

Roeder, K. 2021. 'Charles Lang Freer, Whistler and The Balcony', paper presented at the 'Whistler, Nature and Industry' symposium, University of Glasgow, 5 November.

Roodenburg, H., ed. 2014. *A Cultural History of the Senses in the Renaissance, 1450–1650*, Vol. 3 of *A Cultural History of the Senses*, 6 vols., C. Classen, ed. (London: Bloomsbury).

Rubin, W., ed. 1984. *'Primitivism' in Modern Art: Affinity of the Tribal and the Modern, Vol. I*, 2 vols. (New York: Museum of Modern Art).

Salter, C. 2022. *Sensing Machines: How Sensors Shape Our Everyday Life* (Cambridge, MA: MIT Press).

Santos, B. de Sousa. 2002. *Toward a New Legal Common Sense: Law, Globalization, and Emancipation* (London: Butterworths).

Santos, B. de Sousa. 2018. *The End of the Cognitive Empire: The Coming of Age of Epistemologies of the South* (Durham, NC: Duke University Press).

Sarasohn, L. T. 2003. 'Leviathan and the lady', in *Authorial Conquests: Essays on Genre in the Writings of Margaret Cavendish*, L. Cottegnies and N. Weitz, eds., 40–58 (London: Associated University Presses).

Sarasohn, L. T. 2009. 'A science turned upside down: Feminism and the natural philosophy of Margaret Cavendish', *Ashgate Critical Essays on Women Writers in England, 1550–1700, Vol. 7: Margaret Cavendish*, S. H. Mendelson, ed., 133–51 (Farnham: Ashgate).

Sarukkai, S. 2014. 'Unity of the senses in Indian thought', in *Exploring the Senses*, A. Michaels and C. Wulf, eds., 297–308 (London: Routledge).

Schiebinger, L. 1989. *The Mind Has No Sex? Women in the Origins of Modern Science* (Cambridge, MA: Harvard University Press).

Schillmeier, M., R. Stock and B. Ochsner. 2023. 'Introduction – Techniques of hearing: Histories, practices, and acoustic experiences', in *Techniques of Hearing: History, Theory and Practices*, M. Schillmeier, R. Stock and B. Ochsner, eds., 1–12 (Abingdon: Routledge).

Schulz, M. 2023. 'Listening or reading? Rethinking ableism in relation to the senses and (acoustic) text', in *Techniques of Hearing: History, Theory and Practices*, M. Schillmeier, R. Stock and B. Ochsner, eds., 102–13 (Abingdon: Routledge).

Schurig, E. 2023. 'Mobile music listening and the self-management of health and well-being', in *Techniques of Hearing: History, Theory and Practices*, M. Schillmeier, R. Stock and B. Ochsner, eds., 66–76 (Abingdon: Routledge).

Seeger, A. [1988] 2004. *Why Suyá Sing* (Champaign: University of Illinois Press).

Sennett, R. 1977. *The Fall of Public Man* (New York: Alfred A. Knopf).

Sennett, R. 1994. *Flesh and Stone: The Body and the City in Western Civilization* (New York: W. W. Norton & Co.).

Seremetakis, C. N. 1994. *The Senses Still* (Chicago, IL: University of Chicago Press).

Seremetakis, C. N. 2019. *Sensing the Everyday* (Abingdon: Routledge).

Serres, M. 2009. *The Five Senses: A Philosophy of Mingled Bodies* (London: Continuum).

Shapiro, L. and S. Spaulding. 2021. 'Embodied cognition', in *The Stanford Encyclopedia of Philosophy*, E. N. Zalta, ed., https://plato.stanford.edu/arch ives/win2021/entries/embodied-cognition/.

Shaw-Miller, S. 2013. *Eye hEar: The Visual in Music* (London: Routledge).

Shiga, J. 2017. 'An empire of sound: Sentience, sonar and sensory impudence', in *Sensing Law*, S. N. Hamilton, D. Majury, D. Moore, N. Sargent and C. Wilke, eds., 238–56 (New York: Routledge).

Siegfried, B. R. 2003. 'Anecdotal and cabalistic forms in *Observations upon Experimental Philosophy*', in *Authorial Conquests: Essays on Genre in the Writings of Margaret Cavendish*, L. Cottegnies and N. Weitz, eds., 59–79 (London: Associated University Presses).

Siegfried, B. R. 2006. 'Dining at the table of sense: Shakespeare, Cavendish, and *The Convent of Pleasure*', in *Cavendish and Shakespeare*

Interconnections, K. Romack and J. Fitzmaurice, eds., 63–84 (Aldershot: Ashgate).

Siegfried, B. R. and L. T. Sarasohn. 2014. *God and Nature in the Thought of Margaret Cavendish* (Abingdon: Routledge).

Siegfried, B. R. and L. Walters. 2022. 'Introduction', in *Margaret Cavendish: An Interdisciplinary Perspective*, L. Walters and B. R. Siegfried, eds., 1–15 (Cambridge: Cambridge University Press).

Siewert, J. 2004. 'Art, music, and an aesthetics of place in Whistler's Nocturne paintings', in *Turner, Whistler, Monet: Impressionist Visions*, K. Lochnan, ed., 141–62 (London: Tate Publishing).

Simmel, G. [1907] 1997. 'Sociology of the senses', in *Simmel on Culture: Selected Writings* (London: Sage).

Smart, A. and J. Smart. 2017. *Posthumanism* (Toronto: University of Toronto Press).

Smith, M. M. 2021. *A Sensory History Manifesto* (University Park: Pennsylvania State University Press).

Smith, M. M. 2022. 'All the buzz: Why bees mattered in the Civil War', in *Animal Histories in the Civil War Era*, E. Hess, ed., 121–34 (Baton Rouge: Louisiana State University Press).

SNAPSHOT. 1996. *Super Senses* (n.p.: DK Publishing).

Spence, C. 2018. 'Crossmodal correspondences: A synopsis', in *Senses and Sensation: Critical and Primary Sources, Vol. 3: Biology, Psychology and Neuroscience*, D. Howes, ed., 91–132 (Abingdon: Routledge).

Spence, C. 2021. *Sensehacking* (New York: Penguin Random House).

Spöhrer, M. 2023. 'Binaural gaming arrangements: Techno-sensory configurations of playing the audio game *A Blind Legend*', in *Techniques of Hearing: History, Theory and Practices*, M. Schillmeier, R. Stock and B. Ochsner, eds., 114–24 (Abingdon: Routledge).

Stevens, M. 2021. *Secret Worlds: The Extraordinary Senses of Animals* (Oxford: Oxford University Press).

Stevenson, J. 2009. 'The mechanist-vitalist soul of Margaret Cavendish', in *Ashgate Critical Essays on Women Writers in England, 1550–1700, Vol. 7: Margaret Cavendish*, S. H. Mendelson, ed., 153–69 (Farnham: Ashgate).

Stock, R. 2023. 'Hearing echoes as an audile technique', in *Techniques of Hearing: History, Theory and Practices*, M. Schillmeier, R. Stock and B. Ochsner, eds., 55–65 (Abingdon: Routledge).

Sullivan, L. 1986. 'Sound and senses', *History of Religions*, 26(1): 1–33.

Sutherland, D. E. 2014. *Whistler: A Life for Art's Sake* (New Haven, CT: Yale University Press).

Sur, M. 2004. 'Rewiring cortex: Cross-modal plasticity and its implications for cortical development and function', in *The Handbook of Multisensory Processes*, G. Calvert, C. Spence and B. Stein, eds., 681–94 (Cambridge, MA: MIT Press).

Tahhan, D. A. 2015. 'The Japanese touch', *The Senses and Society*, 9(1): 92–8.

Tallis, R. 2011. *Aping Mankind: Neuromania, Darwinitis and the Misrepresentation of Humanity* (Durham, NC: Acumen).

Teniswood-Harvey, A. 2006. Colour-music: Musical modelling in James McNeill Whistler's art, unpublished PhD dissertation, University of Tasmania.

Thoreau, H. D. 1906. *The Writings of Henry David Thoreau*, 20 vols. (Boston, MA: Houghton Mifflin).

Thurschwell, P. 2001. *Literature, Technology and Magical Thinking, 1880–1920* (Cambridge: Cambridge University Press).

Toner, J. P., ed. 2014. *A Cultural History of the Senses in Antiquity, 500 BCE–500 CE*, Vol. 1 of *A Cultural History of the Senses*, 6 vols., C. Classen, ed. (London: Bloomsbury).

van Campen, C. 2010. *The Hidden Sense: Synaesthesia in Art and Science* (Cambridge, MA: MIT Press).

van Campen, C. 2014. *The Proust Effect: The Senses as Doorways to Lost Memories* (Oxford: Oxford University Press).

Vannini P., D. Waskul and S. Gottschalk. 2012. *The Senses in Self, Society and Culture: A Sociology of the Senses* (New York: Routledge).

Varela, F. J., E. Rosch and E. Thompson. [1991] 2017. *The Embodied Mind: Cognitive Science and Human Experience* (Cambridge, MA: MIT Press).

Velasco, C. and M. Obrist. 2020. *Multisensory Experiences* (Oxford: Oxford University Press).

Vila, A., ed. 2014. *A Cultural History of the Senses in the Age of Enlightenment, 1650–1800*, Vol. 4 of *A Cultural History of the Senses*, 6 vols., C. Classen, ed. (London: Bloomsbury).

Vinge, L. 1975. 'Chapman's *Ovids Banquet of Sence*: Its sources and theme', *Journal of the Warburg and Courtauld Institutes*, 38(1): 234–57.

von Uexküll, J. 2018. 'The theory of meaning', in *Senses and Sensation: Critical and Primary Sources, Vol. 3: Biology, Psychology and Neuroscience*, D. Howes, ed., 49–74 (Abingdon: Routledge).

Walters, L. 2009. 'Gender subversion in the science of Margaret Cavendish', in *Ashgate Critical Essays on Women Writers in England, 1550–1700, Vol. 7: Margaret Cavendish*, S. H. Mendelson, ed., 251–62 (Farnham: Ashgate).

Watson, L. 1999. *Jacobson's Organ and the Remarkable Nature of Smell* (London: Allen Lane).

Whitaker, K. 2003. *Mad Madge* (London: Chatto & Windus).

Willkomm, J. and A. Boersma. 2023. 'Hearing like an animal: Exploring acoustic experience beyond human ears', in *Techniques of Hearing: History, Theory and Practices*, M. Schillmeier, R. Stock and B. Ochsner, eds., 125–38 (Abingdon: Routledge).

Willsdon, C. 2018. 'Nature on the margins: Parks, gardens, and coasts in Whistler's work of the 1880s and 90s', in P. de Montfort and C. Willsdon, *Whistler and Nature*, 77–111 (London: Paul Holberton).

Willsdon, C. 2019a. 'Sounding the garden: Whistler, Darwin and music', online video clip, www.youtube.com/watch?v=aF1MooaFHdQ.

Willsdon, C. 2019b. '"The lady of the garden, lawn and blackbird": Beatrix Whistler and horticulture', *Women's History*, 2(13): 15–22.

Wilmerding, J. 1989. *American Light: The Luminist Movement 1850–1875* (Princeton, NJ: Princeton University Press).

Yong, E. 2020. *An Immense World: How Animal Senses Reveal the Hidden Realms Around Us* (London: Bodley Head).

Young, D. 2005. 'The smell of greenness: Cultural synaesthesia in the Western Desert', *Etnofoor*, 18(1): 61–77.

Ziefert, H. 2014. *You Can't Taste a Pickle With Your Ear!* (Maplewood, NJ: Blue Apple Books).

Zika, F. 2018. 'Colour and sound: Transcending the limits of the senses', in *Senses and Sensation: Critical and Primary Sources, Vol. 2: History and Sociology*, D. Howes, ed., 303–16 (Abingdon: Routledge).

Acknowledgements

I wish to thank the founding editor of the Elements in Histories of Emotions and the Senses series, Jan Plamper, and the series editors Mark Smith, Rob Boddice and Piroska Nagy, for their enthusiastic support for this Element project, the two anonymous reviewers for their appreciation of this manuscript, and my editor at Cambridge University Press, Liz Friend-Smith and her staff, for seeing it through the review process and production. My deepest debt, as always, is to Constance Classen for the inspiring example of her own work in the history of the senses. I am otherwise grateful to my family, students and colleagues for their good humour and sharp insights as I have engaged them in puzzling over the senses together with me for going on 30 years.

Section 1 was first published as the foreword to *Techniques of Hearing*, at the invitation of the book's editors Michael Schillmeier, Robert Stock and Beate Ochsner (2023). Section 2 was first presented at the interdisciplinary symposium held in conjunction with the exhibition *Belle Haleine: The Scent of Art* at the Museum Tinguley, Basel, in April 2015 and published in the accompanying catalogue. I wish to thank Routledge in the first case, and the Director of the Tinguely, Roland Wetzel, in the second, for permission to reuse this material. I should note that both sections have been revised substantially for inclusion in this Element.

Section 6 began as a keynote address (delivered via Zoom) at the 'Whistler, Nature and Industry' symposium, organized by Clare Willsdon and Patricia de Montfort of the Department of Art History at the University Glasgow, in October 2021. The section has profited greatly from their commentaries.

Cambridge Elements ⹀

Histories of Emotions and the Senses

Series Editors

Rob Boddice
Tampere University

Rob Boddice (PhD, FRHistS) is Senior Research Fellow at the Academy of Finland Centre of Excellence in the History of Experiences. He is the author/editor of thirteen books, including *Knowing Pain: A History of Sensation, Emotion and Experience* (Polity Press, 2023), *Humane Professions: The Defence of Experimental Medicine, 1876–1914* (Cambridge University Press, 2021) and *A History of Feelings* (Reaktion, 2019).

Piroska Nagy
Université du Québec à Montréal (UQAM)

Piroska Nagy is Professor of Medieval History at the Université du Québec à Montréal (UQAM) and initiated the first research program in French on the history of emotions. She is the author or editor of fourteen volumes, including *Le Don des larmes au Moyen Âge* (Albin Michel, 2000); *Medieval Sensibilities: A History of Emotions in the Middle Ages, with Damien Boquet* (Polity, 2018); and *Histoire des émotions collectives: Épistémologie, émergences, expériences*, with D. Boquet and L. Zanetti Domingues (Classiques Garnier, 2022).

Mark Smith
University of South Carolina

Mark Smith (PhD, FRHistS) is Carolina Distinguished Professor of History and Director of the Institute for Southern Studies at the University of South Carolina. He is author or editor of over a dozen books and his work has been translated into Chinese, Korean, Danish, German, and Spanish. He has lectured in Europe, throughout the United States, Australia, and China and his work has been featured in the New York Times, the London Times, the Washington Post, and the Wall Street Journal. He serves on the US Commission for Civil Rights.

About the Series

Born of the emotional and sensory "turns," Elements in Histories of Emotions and the Senses move one of the fastest-growing interdisciplinary fields forward. The series is aimed at scholars across the humanities, social sciences, and life sciences, embracing insights from a diverse range of disciplines, from neuroscience to art history and economics. Chronologically and regionally broad, encompassing global, transnational, and deep history, it concerns such topics as affect theory, intersensoriality, embodiment, human–animal relations, and distributed cognition. The founding editor of the series was Jan Plamper.

Cambridge Elements ≡

Histories of Emotions and the Senses

A full series listing is available at: www.cambridge.org/EHES

Printed in the United States
by Baker & Taylor Publisher Services